Winning Doubles

Winning Doubles

✦

Mastering Outdoor Volleyball Through Strategy and Training

Jennifer Sangiacomo

iUniverse, Inc.

New York Lincoln Shanghai

Winning Doubles
Mastering Outdoor Volleyball Through Strategy and Training

iUniverse books may be ordered through booksellers or by contacting:

iUniverse
2021 Pine Lake Road, Suite 100
Lincoln, NE 68512
www.iuniverse.com
1-800-Authors (1-800-288-4677)

Because of the dynamic nature of the Internet, any Web addresses
or links contained in this book may have changed
since publication and may no longer be valid.

ISBN: 978-0-595-45863-9 (pbk)
ISBN: 978-0-595-90165-4 (ebk)

Printed in the United States of America

Contents

Acknowledgements

Thank you to my father, Alan Sangiacomo, for helping with the editing process. Special thanks to Tim Stewart, my content editor, and fiancé whose advice over the years I have valued both on and off the court.

1

Introduction

I guess I should start by giving you a little bit about my experience and background. Hopefully, this won't bore you too badly!

I began playing doubles when I was 18. At that point, I had been playing indoor volleyball for six years. By then, I went to college at Nazareth College, a small Division 3 school in Rochester, NY. To call my playing career up through my college years mediocre would be considered a very generous characterization. Indoors, I was an average player, especially when you consider I was "only" 5-feet 5-inches. I was not much of an offensive threat, and my passing and defense was not really what it should have been to make up for what I was lacking in other areas.

What I always had was athleticism, a great serve, and an even better work ethic. When I first set foot on the doubles' court in the summer of 1997, I quickly realized that those three qualities would be a great springboard to a successful playing career outdoors. After my first outdoor doubles tournament, I was floored by what I could do—especially on offense. I never imagined I could have so much fun and still become successful at volleyball.

That potential made me want to challenge myself and learn more about the game. The more I played, the more I truly started to enjoy the sport of volleyball and appreciate all the intricacies of the game. Doubles provides so many more opportunities to pass, set, hit, serve, and play defense. It also physically conditions an athlete. It's not easy to master all of these things, and that is why playing doubles—and playing it well—is such a great feeling!

As I gained more experience and knowledge playing outdoor volleyball, my indoor game also improved. At the same time, I have traveled the grass doubles' circuit in the Northeast and have won Open Level Tournaments on both grass and sand in New York, Maryland, Virginia, Connecticut and Massachusetts. Not to mention, I have won thousands of dollars playing in tournaments. Not bad for an amateur!

The more I played, the more I developed a passion for the sport. I became involved not just as a player, but also as an organizer and coach. I have run doubles tournaments for Capital District Grass Doubles in the Albany, NY area for the past seven years—the last five of which I have been an AVPNext promoter. I have also coached for Primo Volleyball Club and Lakeside Volleyball Club, which has been the most dominant high school program in the state of New York for the last decade. Currently, I am an assistant coach for the women's volleyball team at Siena College and I'm proud to say that the team earned a bid to the NCAA Tournament for the past two seasons after having suffered through three straight losing seasons prior to 2005. Ten years ago, I could not have possibly imagined having all of these opportunities in the sport I loved playing so much.

Given my experiences thus far, I have been blessed to meet, coach, watch and play against some great players and have been truly privileged to see the sport from all perspectives. Without my success at doubles, I may not have had many of these opportunities.

Anyone with enough interest in the sport to read this book knows that outdoor and indoor volleyball is different in so many ways. The best indoor players can play outdoor doubles—and they may lose pretty badly to a core of players they normally beat on a 6's court. There are many reasons for this. Mainly, it's because doubles is game of strategy and conditioning where each player on the court must be well rounded and is able to execute each skill well. While a 6-foot 4-inch player might dominate the middle hitter position and be a huge block, that same player on the doubles court may not have strong enough passing skills to compete because that player may rarely play the back row.

Nevertheless, you are reading this book for at least one of a few main reasons. Perhaps you are a great indoor player trying to make a successful transition. Maybe you currently are playing doubles and are looking for some pointers to take you to the next level, or to get the winning edge at the level at which you are currently playing. Regardless, the goal of this book is to help you improve all facets of your game.

Throughout the years, as I have tried to get better I have searched for books and articles on how to improve my doubles game. I have learned a great amount of information on virtually every topic—from basic skills, to improving my vertical, to visualization. One thing that increasingly became clear as I improved was that there was little literature geared to the very good or expert player. I would purchase books that claimed to improve your doubles game, but find I already knew most or all of the information in the book.

As I continue my search for good sources of information, I'm finding most books largely focus on the fundamentals and include information that is common sense to even a beginning player. Better books may include some drills. But have you noticed at tournaments that you play in, that the best players do not always win? In fact, a team may be a heavy favorite or the considered "best" at a given tournament, but still lose. To consistently win, a team must possess more than just strong fundamentals.

While the execution of certain skills will be briefly discussed, this book is intended for players who already exhibit the fundamentals. The purpose is not to teach the basic skills, as there is enough literature already out there, but to give pointers on how to refine those skills, incorporate different techniques, styles and strategies, and then to use them to your advantage. My primary goal is to provide you with information on the nuances of the game—strategy in particular—that many books omit. I call it "the game within the game," and I believe that the strategies presented in this book paired with your commitment to winning will be the difference in your success!

2

Partnering Up: Choosing a Partner

Depending on your playing goals, what you look for in a partner is going to differ. It is my assumption that if you are reading this book, then your goal is to be competitive and, most likely, become as successful as you can. Using that reasoning, there are definite factors you should consider when choosing a partner. Before I start, you should realize that forming a winning combination is not an overnight process. A key component of partnership is chemistry and trust and both partners must be willing to work toward those goals. You also need to know that you will most likely go through several partners before you feel things start to click with any one partner. Even after that, you may find yourself ready for someone new. Here, in no particular order, are the main things you should look for in a potential partner:

#1 Find a partner who has similar goals

One important part of playing volleyball is having fun. For some people, this comes before winning. For others, it is not fun unless you are winning. Having a partner who does not share in your philosophy will not translate into fun. Let's say you are playing to win, but your partner is just happy to be out on a nice day. Chances are that you will not react to things in the same way because of your different expectations regarding what will make a successful day. This will create tension.

Here's another example: Partner A and B are playing against people they know and one of the people on the other side of the net is a much weaker player. Partner A, wanting to win, obviously is going to serve that player. Partner B, however, either through guilt or trying to be nice, is not serving aggressively or simply choosing to serve the stronger player—allowing the other team to earn points more easily. Think of how frustrating that would be to both partners. Partner A would be upset at the lost opportunities, and Partner B would be upset by Partner A's "cutthroat" attitude.

Given this, the most important piece of advice in choosing a partner is finding out his/her goals. You do not need to agree on every single philosophy and goal, but you should agree on the ones that you both consider most important. The hardest part about this is actually finding out this information. This will be addressed in point number seven.

It may be helpful for you to write down some of your personal goals and philosophies to assess what is important. It is also fun to look back at these at a later date to see if, and how, they have changed.

_____

_____

_____

_____

_____

_____

#2 Opposites attract

It may seem like this point contradicts my first point. However, on some things, partners should have differences as a way to complement each other's game.

I have played with many different partners over my career and I always try to find someone who has a game that is similar to mine in style, but who also brings something to the game that I do not. As an example, perhaps you are an aggressive server and try to get points by forcing bad passes. Given this style, you need a partner who is going to serve consistently, getting a high percentage of their serves in the court. If both partners are highly aggressive from the serving line, there is likely to be a lot of service errors. If your partner does miss a lot of serves, you have to think twice and consider not being equally aggressive when serving. That cramps your style by taking you off your game. Having a partner who brings the serving consistency would allow you to stay aggressive and still maximize your skills.

As I said in my introduction, I'm short in comparison to other athletes in the sport, especially at the Open Level. Because of my height disadvantage, I need a couple things out of a partner in order to play my best and win against opponents who are physically bigger than I am. For starters, I need a taller partner to carry the blocking load, so I can scurry around and play defense. Second, because of my height, I am, most likely, going to be receiving the majority of serves and then be facing a block. Therefore, I need a partner who can set accurately and who can communicate. My partner must call out shots, so I can work my way past a big block in front of me.

Now, it's your turn. Brainstorm your strengths and limitations, and determine what type of qualities your partner should have to maximize your strengths and make up for your limitations, so as to complement you game. You also might want to think about your partner's strengths and weaknesses, and what parts of your game you need to do to work on to maximize your partner's strengths and make up for his or her weaknesses.

Strengths	Skills Needed to Complement Yours
Ex. I am a strong, aggressive server 1. 2.	Ex. I need a partner with a consistent serve 1. 2.
Limitations	Skills Needed to Complement Yours
Ex. I am shorter than my opponents 1. 2.	Ex. I need a taller partner for blocking duties 1. 2.

#3 Match Making

In my experience, I have seen successful partnerships form in one of two ways. The first, and most common, is that both partners played together or against each other in a lower level until they achieved consistent success, and then moved up together to the next level to start the learning process at the higher level. The less common way, of course, is a player from a higher level taking a new partner under his or her wing, so to speak. The higher skilled the higher-level player, the easier the transition.

One key to remember is that it is important to pair with someone who plays at least as well as you. The last thing you want to do is team with someone who is at a lower level. That may sound harsh, but, if you want to win, it's an absolute truth. If you choose a weaker partner, you may then be forced to compete at a lower level than your skill level and, in the long run, this will not help you improve your game. Also, you may not be competitive as a team and you may become frustrated because I can almost guarantee that your opponent will mostly serve to your weaker partner.

On the other hand, if your partner is much stronger, you are going to have a lot of pressure to side-out, as you will get most of the serves. You might embrace this pressure if you can handle the added stress of getting served every ball and having to hit. Ultimately, these added reps would only improve your game.

However, if you are struggling and having a hard time dealing with that pressure, you may want to change your partner to someone more equal to your skill. That is why it is important to have a partner that complements you. For instance, you may have a hard time siding-out, but your partner might be good at taking the ball over on two to relieve some of this pressure. Having a partnership where both partners pose threats also keeps the opponent guessing and off-balance. And, your opponent has a more difficult decision when choosing to whom to serve.

When in doubt on choosing a partner, however, if you have a choice, you should always err on the side of having a stronger partner. You will learn more this way and it will keep you more competitive.

#4 Find a partner that is willing to improve his or her game

Life is too short to make the same mistake more than once. The same is true of your playing career. It is vital to your success to improve your areas of weakness and to keep fine-tuning your game. Any player looking to improve needs to commit to that, and, in the same way, so does a team. There is no substitute for hard work.

Let's say you and your partner just lost a tournament because the ball was continually set too tight, allowing the opponent to block the ball. Hopefully, you recognized this was a flaw in your game and took steps to correct it prior to your next tournament. You ran into two problems:

1. You didn't know how to set up each other with a block, and

2. You didn't know what to do after the bad set was executed.

Realistically, you need to be able to practice the skills of setting and the arts of communicating what shots to hit, and then covering—should your partner still get blocked. In a situation like this, would your partner practice this with you before the next tournament? Can you both play pickup games during the week? Committing to improvement is important in advancing through skill levels. If this is your goal, make sure your partner shares that goal.

#5 Can you communicate?

Great teams have trust and chemistry. That comes from communication. Communication can be in the form of giving your partner a call as he or she is hitting, or it can also be some constructive criticism about the locations of your partner's passes, etc. Even the best teams have things they need to talk about at some point.

Partners should be honest with one other and also be open to what the other has to say. You can't have a partner who is too sensitive because that person may just feel hurt by your comments and not really listen. You may be playing with someone who is incredibly talented, but also very insecure. Perhaps you want to comment about the sets you have been getting, but when you request that your sets be tighter, instead of getting what you ask, the sets only get worse. I am sure at some point this has happened to you or will happen to you. If your partner takes comments like these as a personal attack, you will not have a good outcome.

Some partners will deal better with a comment such as "I would be able to hit better if the set was closer," instead of, "You are setting me too far off the net." How you say things is a personal choice, and many of you might have chosen to go with the former option.

When I am playing in a tournament, I am a straight shooter and do not want to take the time or energy to sugarcoat things. Little communication quirks, while small, but common, can cause a partnership not to work. It is essential to be able to communicate honestly and openly without affecting a partner's play.

The last thing you want is a partner who gets offended by constructive criticism and takes things personally. When you first select a partner, get a feel for how that person responds to suggestions and criticism. You might want to consider, based on your partner, when and how to offer suggestions. Some people do not like to be told what to do, or how to do it in the middle of the game. Some need things downplayed. Remember, this is a two-way street, so let your partner know to be open with you as well.

Some things to think about: What is your communication style? How do you prefer to receive and deliver suggestions and criticism during the course of a game?

_____

_____

_____

_____

_____

_____

#6 Be Flexible

An obvious aspect of finding a partner is choosing the side you play. If you like to play strong side (hit and pass from the left side of the court), then you need a partner who can or will, play the opposite side. If you are unwilling to play both sides, you are severely narrowing your choices.

In high school I was an outside hitter. Naturally, when I started playing doubles after my senior year, I wanted to play the left side. During my first couple of years, I would only play that side. Despite that preference, an elite open player who only played the strong side still asked me to team up for a tournament. What to do?

I had reached the point where I wanted to play at the open level, as I was currently having a lot of success at the "A" level. My partner and I planned on moving up to the open level, but we both figured we would have a rough transition and that it would take time to grow. I also knew this player was the best open player in our area. I wasn't about to pass up this opportunity by refusing to play the weak side.

I thought I would have a tough tournament because I knew I would be getting the majority of the serves. My partner was an incredible setter and made it easy for me to sideout and transition to a new side. Not only did we win that tournament, but also won many more together that summer and years later are still winning when we occasionally team up, despite the fact I have to play out of my supposed element. Since then, I have practiced playing both sides and I have been fortunate to play with some great players and win both women's and mixed tournaments. Had I not been flexible, I would not have had the opportunity and privilege to play with these partners.

In addition to making yourself more marketable, another benefit of having the ability to play both sides is that there is a good chance in a game you may have to hit from the other side. You might be a left-side player but, if you make a dig on the right side, a set will be on that side, as well. Also, you have the advantages of the ability to give your opponent a different look when serve receiving by switching sides and the opportunity to gain more perspective that may help you learn more about the game in terms of positioning, strategy and reading your opponent. So, next time you play pickup games, consider trying to play the "other side."

#7 The Dating Game

Chances are you know who your ideal partner is, but that person already has a partner, or may be hesitant about taking you as a partner. Asking someone to play is just like asking someone out on a date. No one wants to be rejected!

Hopefully you have enough savvy not to ask someone above your league to make a commitment. If you play BB and usually finish .500, it would be quite a stretch to ask someone who consistently makes the finals in A, a higher level. Instead, you might consider asking a player at your level who consistently makes the playoffs. That move might be just what you need to bring your game up a notch.

While no one person is going to be all of the things you read in #'s 1-6, you probably now have a better idea of who might be on your list of potential partners. In the last chapter you will find some additional thoughts on this. For now, though, enthusiasm and hustle go a long way! People are more likely to want to play with you if they know that they will have a good time and that you are going to give it your all.

#8 Techniques and Fundamentals

This may very well be the most obvious, yet important, part of choosing a partner. So, it is fitting that is the last, but certainly not the least, important thing to consider when looking for a potential partner.

You need to make sure that the partner you choose has at least average ball control compared to yourself and others in your level of play. If your potential partner is a great passer but can not get his or her serve over the net, then that is something he or she needs to work out on his or her own before playing tournaments. That player simply does not have the fundamentals needed for tournament play.

That doesn't mean they can't acquire the technique through hard work, but you will only be frustrated and will gain little from the experience until that happens.

A more practical example would concern setting. As you progress up through levels of play, it is expected that your ball control will improve. In BB for instance, it is not the standard that there is always bump, set and spike. It isn't unusual for the ball to be contacted only one or two times before it is sent over the net. In some cases, passing the ball does not guarantee that you will hit. In the A level it is the norm for all three contacts to be used, although the set may not always be in the same place each time. At the Open level, all three contacts are used and sets should be consistent.

Therefore, if you are playing A and are a good passer, but your partner is setting you ten feet off the net, or twenty feet high, then that partner obviously does not have the ball control to be playing at that level or with you.

So, as you search for a partner, make sure that your fundamentals and ball control are equivalent and that they also match up with other opponents at that level. Otherwise, you are in for a long day of bad sets—and bad games—while you look on helplessly as your partner gets every single serve.

Final Thoughts

Some of you may be wondering how important it is to play with the same person. In lower levels, there tends to be a revolving door of partners. Sometimes, it seems like you will see a certain player with a new partner at every tournament. You will also notice that, at these levels, a different team usually wins each tournament.

However, at the upper levels it is far more common to play with the same partner throughout a season. That is why at those levels the same teams tend to do well time and time again. Those teams have established consistency and trust, and have learned to play with one another.

It is also true that players can have success playing with different partners. In fact, as players move up through the ranks, they play with a wide range of partners before figuring out which best complements their game. Early in a player's career, experience may be an important factor in selecting a partner, but as a player gains experience, that may become a less valued trait.

As you move up and improve, I encourage you to play with different people for many reasons. In addition to learning to build team chemistry, you will become aware of what type of partner suits you the best. Undoubtedly, as you and your partner get better, you will either grow together, or apart. If you do not complement each other, inevitably you will need to find a partner who does.

A few years ago, there was a team that consistently came to play in tournaments I was running. They made the finals in the "A" level, time and time again, winning in most of their appearances. Neither was an intimidating hitter. They also were both small, so neither player blocked. They both placed the ball very well and played solid defense. They seldom made mistakes and always were able to pass, set and hit each play. In essence, they put it on their opponents to make the mistakes using their ball control as an advantage. When they made the transition to Open, they were still able to do well, but rarely make playoffs! The reason for this is because their strengths were now their weaknesses. At the lower level they were accustomed to sending the ball over the net and it resulting in a point. When they used this passive approach at the Open level, these shots were tracked down by faster and bigger opponents, who had the same, if not more, ball control than they did. They also were not able to play defense as well because without a block, they could not stop the offensive powerhouses at that level.

Both players would surely have success if they teamed up with a different partner.

Likewise, there will be times where you may decide to form a new partnership, whether it be to play a different side, form a better combination, team up with a better setter or blocker. Whatever the case, there should be no hard feelings about that as it is part of the game. Your ultimate goal should be to put out the most competitive effort that you can.

3

Live by the Serve, Die by the Serve

More than any other skill, serving has the possibility to instantly change the nature of the game. A good server can create a bad pass that will lead to a dig and scoring opportunity. A great server will put runs of points together that can either bring a team back, or put them ahead and seal the game. It is important to see serving as another way to attack the game and to tilt things in your favor.

There are three types of servers:

1. There are those who just try to put the ball in play—the "Lolli-poppers." They do not always think about whom they are serving to, how hard, or the type of serve and generally they take no risks. They are playing it safe. These players tend to be docile, only wanting to get the ball in the court. They are afraid of making mistakes and hope their opponents make the mistakes. They are not thinking about controlling the flow of the game. Rather, they are along for the ride and let their opponent dictate the course of the game and fire the first shot. The meek may inherit the earth, but they do not win sporting events! Remember that as you read this chapter and as you play the game.

2. Then there are the "Master Strategists," who focus more on serving a particular spot on the court that would make it hard for their opponent to sideout. They are not content to simply serve at a certain player. Rather, they try to serve to a spot that will make it difficult for their opponent to pass well. For example, the server may know that a particular player has difficulty with a float serve, or perhaps a player may have trouble with serves that are deep and to the left. The aim of this style of serving is to expose weaknesses in the opponents' serve receive and force opposing teams pass serves that they are not comfortable handling.

3. Last, there are players who are intent on serving the ball as hard as they can. These players—the "Bombers"—can have runs of aces, or runs of errors. With this type of player it is all or nothing, ace or error. They are quite content with the latter as long at they hit the ball hard.

There is much to be learned from each style of serving. There will be times in the game where you do just have to get your serve in the court. While you do this, however, you may still have to mix in some of the other styles. This is because as you play harder opponents if you serve only lollipops you will give the other team a better chance to pass, set and hit.

So what is the correct style? The answer depends on you and your comfort level. I would never—under ANY circumstance—recommend serving just to get it in play. Aggression pays off and the service line should be seen as a place where you can attack the game and keep your opponents from getting into an offensive rhythm. Creating a bad pass, more often than not, will lead to a less ideal set, which in turn will make the attack more predictable. This is one example of a way to use an offensive skill in order to improve your defensive chances. You always should have a plan, which can be as simple as serving as much as possible to a certain player.

Personally, I am a big proponent of putting as much pressure on your opponent as possible and challenging them with my serve. I may try to serve hard down the middle, or to the deep corners. I do risk making serving errors, but these risks often result in rewards. I will start the game with this in mind. If that strategy results in too many errors, then I adjust my level of aggressiveness accordingly, hoping to be able to turn it back up later if I get into a groove.

If you are serving too many balls out, that takes a lot of pressure off of the other team. Always make an opponent earn their points. Playing this way, I have won a lot of games against players that probably should have beaten my team. In fact, I credit this skill as the single most important factor as to why I have been successful.

So, what are other reasons why you want to be aggressive? One big reason is because it is the first chance your team has to attack the game. Many people think that an aggressive serve, by nature, is fast in speed and lacks control on the part of the server. However, when I serve aggressively, I'm trying to go after an opponent and keep them off balance. So, you can improve your game by serving to spots from where your opponents have difficulty passing. For instance, you may have decided that you are only going to serve the left side player, but this does not mean you should serve it right to them so that they only have to worry about hitting!

Another aggressive strategy is always trying to make the passer move in order to pass. Serve the ball deep and make your opponent decide whether or not to play the ball, and whether to play it overhead or move back for it. One of the most difficult balls to pass is a deep ball over the shoulders. It can be hard to judge whether or not the ball is "in" and it is also awkward to move backwards. After a few times serving that spot, receivers will begin to move back to give themselves an advantage.

Once you see this shift, you can now start serving short. By doing this you are creating room for yourself by establishing a deep serve, forcing your opponent to respect your deep game. When you begin serving short your opponent has to start playing a guessing game. You can also serve balls into the middle to create space on the line to serve to, which will create more confusion and second-guessing on the part of your opponent. As your spot serving gets more accurate you can mix it up and not just settle for serving to the weaker player. Now, you are really going after both players, keeping them on their toes and making them focus on passing.

Serving Spots

Whether you are serving hard or not, placement is always important. You can serve the ball as hard as you want, but if it is right at an opponent then your serve will be easy to pass. In fact, that only makes them feel more confident they can pass your future serves. Instead, to improve your serving and your overall game, work on serving spots of the court, and work on different types of serves. Remember that a good player has many serving tools, always giving their opponent a new look.

Here are some suggestions of different serves that you should try to make a part of your game:

Spots to Serve

Starting Position	Type of Serve	Where to serve	Why it is a good serve
Any	Top Spin	In the court—aim deep into the wind	Use this serve on windy days. The wind will do most of the work! *(see the section on wind later in this chapter)*

Spots to Serve (Continued)

Starting Position	Type of Serve	Where to serve	Why it is a good serve
Any	Float, Jump Float (Need to have a little pace on this serve!)	Deep or short middle	This makes your opponents have to communicate, and can lead to confusion.
Left/ Right	Float, Top Spin, Jump	Lines (Cross court or line)	Your opponent has to reach outside of their body, move away from their partner, and bring the ball back into the court. A lot of players cheat off their line!
Middle	Float, Top Spin, Jump	Either the extreme left or right of the court. You can also serve middle if your opponents don't cover that area well	By starting in the middle, your opponents may think you are serving the middle of the court, and they are again forced to pass outside of their body
Any	Float, Top Spin, Jump	Deep When you get good at this, try for the corners	This forces your opponents to move back. If they do pass, they have to cover more ground to get up to the net to hit. It may open up the court for a short serve later.

Spots to Serve (Continued)

Starting Position	Type of Serve	Where to serve	Why it is a good serve
Left	Cut for right-handers, slice for left-handers. Strike the ball at 10:00	Toward the right (cross)	Creates confusion as the ball moves away from one player to the other, or away from one player to the line. Harder to pass.
Right	Slice for right-handers, cut for lefthanders Strike the ball at 2:00	Toward the left	Creates confusion as the ball moves away from one player to the other, or away from one player to the line. Harder to pass.

These are the basic spots and type of serves to practice and master. You will find that as time passes you will be able to execute some of these serves better than others. Your goal should be to expand your repertoire, and improve your consistency, so that you are confident attempting different serves during tournaments. As you continue to work on serving, you may even come up with your own patent serve!

Commit to Getting Better

This philosophy goes for all skills, but serving, unlike any other part of the game, is the one area that you can work on by yourself. The more you serve, the more you get a feel of the ball and the court—as well as how you execute serves. To get better, you have to practice. Sometimes, that may entail more than just playing pickup games because players can lose sight of what they are trying to work on. It is often easy to not take pickup seriously, especially when your opponents may not be giving 100 percent, or may not be at your level. It is important to practice the individual skills as much as the actual playing of the game. Therefore, it is also essential that you make time to work on individual skills.

You will have to commit more than just your time and effort, however. You may also need to spend some money. For instance, if you don't already have access to a net and can't borrow one, you may need to purchase a net. A good system runs about $275 and is easy for one person to set up. Then, you'll need to buy a minimum of five or six balls. You can get a quantity discount through most suppliers, or, if you are a resourceful Internet shopper, you can find new and used volleyballs that are inexpensive.

You should set up your net two to three times a week and work on different aspects of your game. However, when working on serving, I'd recommend the following routine. Start by warming up with a five or ten minute jog. Stretch your legs and your shoulders. Then, serve a couple easy rounds of balls—just to loosen up your shoulder. You will notice you will also be conditioning yourself by shagging the balls, which makes it a little more game-like by making you serve after you have just chased!

After you feel warm, identify the types of serves you would like to work on. Serve 10 balls for each type of serve and location. Your goal is to get the ball to the spot you want, the way you want. Keep in mind that this is practice, so you should be aggressive. You can do more repetitions if you think you don't have a good handle for the feel or location of the serve. This will help you get a feel of how you need to hit the ball for it to land in a certain spot. As you do this more, you might start to feel a good enough command that you could hit the serve with your eyes closed!

Another advantage of having that previous success is that you will have confidence in executing serves during an actual game. You will also know which serves still need work and you might not want to try in tournament play. Overall, you will have a great knowledge of yourself, what serve is your most accurate, which is your most consistent and which is your nastiest!

It might be useful to keep track of how many of each type of serve you hit. Then, you can identify which serves you need to work on more. Each year, also try to think of a new serve that you can try to enhance your game and make the practice fun. Here is an example of a practice routine:

Serving Repertoire

From the left side	From the middle	From the right	For fun!
1. Line	1. Left	1. Line	1. Top Spin in the wind
2. Middle	2. Middle	2. Middle	2. Hard as I can!
3. Cross	3. Right	3. Cross	3. Cut Cross from the right
4. Short	4. Short	4. Short	4. Slice Cross from the left
			5. Run in from the right, and cut back to the line

At first, only work on five or six types of serves. Perform 10 repetitions per serve to start. As you progress, you may add more reps or sets so that you are serving 150-170 balls per practice session. Come tournament time, not only will you be conditioned, but will be confident in executing many types of serves. Again, it might be helpful if, after each round, you write down how many serves you attempted, how many were on target, and how many of the ones that were missed were in bounds. Then you can analyze those statistics after a few sessions.

If you do this, you can learn a lot about your serve. You may find that there is a serve that you are not placing where you intended 50 percent of the time, but it is still going into the court. This serve is probably worth trying to use in a real game. Keeping track of your progress this way will help you see which serves you need to develop more and to refrain from using during tournament play. It is not necessary to keep track, but it is useful to see how you are progressing and where you need to improve.

Choosing and Controlling Your Serve

There is much debate over which serve is best. Some people fall in love with the jump serve and its power and ability to intimidate opponents. Some prefer the looks and speed of a topspin serve. Others enjoy making the ball float. So which serve is the most effective? The one you can execute consistently! However, if I had to choose only one, I would pick the floater or the jump float.

Topspin serves are very predictable, and most good players will be able to position themselves in front of the ball and make a good pass. This is because the topspin is not very deceptive. It travels in a set path and is easy to read by any player who watches the ball leave the server's hand. The best time to use topspin is when serving into the wind as the serve will dive when crossing the net, adding a new element of difficulty for your opponents. If you are a natural topspin server, stick with what works.

For non-wind conditions, you still can get some extra movement on your topspin serve. I suggest playing around with your contact of the ball. Practice hitting the ball at 10:00 (a cut for right-handers) or 2:00 (a slice for right-handers) to make the ball cut across the court. When contacting the ball, you hand is completely behind it, making it very difficult for your opponent to identify the path of your serve.

I do encourage all players to work on developing a float serve. It is one of the trickiest serves to pass when executed correctly. No one likes passing a ball that is fluttering and hanging in the air at him or her. Pair this with a jump serve and you can create some major intimidation. You can also gain control of what seems to be the unpredictable motions of a float serve. For this serve, you will change where the ball is positioned on contact.

Surprisingly, many players do not know what makes a serve float and flutter. The answer is the needle hole, where air is put into the ball. This is the heaviest part of the ball, and it is not a coincidence that, when struck, the part of the ball that is heaviest sets the path of the ball's movement. So, if you want your ball to drop, you should contact the ball with the needle facing downward. If you want the ball to float left, the needle should be positioned on the left when the ball is contacted. To do this, you will need to toss the ball without spin so you can control where the needle is positioned on contact. Also, when serving remember not to use your fingers to strike the ball and do not follow through the ball. I encourage you to have some fun playing around with this serve.

Team Serving Strategy

The first decision a team must make is its' serving strategy. As a team, are you going for aces or are you going to try to keep the ball in play? There is a time where both strategies are good ideas. Here are some basic decisions that need to be made before the game is played:

1. *Who are you and your partner going to serve?* Most teams often choose to go after the weaker offensive player. Sometimes it is a good idea to go after the weaker passer. As an example, one season Kerri Walsh and Misty May were steam rolling the competition and had set the record for consecutive matches won on the AVP Tour. Then, they started to lose games—and matches—as opponents switched their strategy. During the winning streak, teams were serving May because she was per-

ceived to be the weaker hitter, when compared to Walsh. Then teams switched up their strategy and started serving Walsh.

The new strategy did two things: One, it threw the rhythm of the team off-balance because May was used to passing and Walsh was used to setting. Two, Walsh was exposed as the weaker passer on the team. This isn't to say Walsh was a bad passer, just that May was used to receiving more serves. Of course, like all good teams, they adjusted and are now again winning tournaments. The lesson here is to remember that just because your opponent may be the better hitter, it doesn't guarantee they are also the better passer. You should also think about the setting ability of both opponents. You may decide to serve the stronger hitter because the partner is not a consistent setter.

2. *Who is going for it and who is the stabilizer?* It is good to be aggressive, because that can pay off with some easy points. However, service errors do come with that aggressiveness so, if both teammates are going for aces, the risk could be too many service errors. The player who has the strongest serve should be the one that takes more chances. That player's partner needs to give the stronger server that opportunity by putting his or her serves in play. You can't continue to try to serve aces if your partner—or you—has missed the last couple of serves.

3. *When is the time and place to go for it?* Don't get me wrong; I am a huge fan of trying to score a quick and easy point off a serve, but there are times when it's best to make sure your serve stays in the court. It would be a lie to tell you that I don't go for an ace every time I serve, but I also spend a lot of time practicing serving in between competitions. I do not recommend that

approach for most players until they have a strong mix of power and control.

There are however, several circumstances where you may decide to "go for it." Some examples: Start off the game aggressively until you have a reason not too be, such as your serve is not on or you are making too many errors. Be more aggressive when you are behind by several points, or take more risks if you have a sizable lead. Remember, you do not want to be so committed to serving hard and getting aces that your opponents get a vacation while you serve every ball out, or in the net. There are points in the game where you need to make your opponent earn a sideout or point. For example, if you miss a serve on game point or in a game that has been tight that is a huge mental break for your opponent.

Which brings me to the point that if you have missed a couple of serves, individually or as a team, you may have to settle for getting your next serve in the court. But, instead of just lobbing it over the net, go with your proven strength. Also, if you are playing a team that is weak offensively, just getting the serve in may be appropriate if you can make digs consistently. There's nothing worse than giving a weak team points off missed serves.

Another time where you should abandon the "ace or nothing" strategy is when weather conditions are poor. I have seen tournaments that are so windy that whichever team got their serve in won the points because the other team could not track the serve or control the ball off the pass.

4. *An exception to the rule.* I never advise a player to serve "safely." However, there will be times that a player can give an opposing team "lollipop" serves, while being tactical at the same time. Mike Dodd and Mike Whitmarsh both had a lot of success on

the AVP Tour, winning several titles. Whitmarsh was not as strong of a defender as Dodd was, but he was an amazing blocker. To maximize their strengths and hide their weaknesses, Whitmarsh was at the net every play to block. Even when Whit served, he would sprint up to the net to set the block. When teams caught on to this strategy, they tried to run a quicker offense, even hitting on two. Basically, they tried to beat Whit to the net so that he could not put up a good block. Therefore, Whit began to serve high lobs to the opponent. With more trajectory creating longer hang time, Whit gave himself the time he needed to get to the net before his opponents set the ball.

If your team needs to make use of a strategy to succeed that is not considered "text book," then don't be afraid to do it—as long as there is a reason behind the method of execution and that method brings success. Be creative in finding the "right way" for your team.

Using the Wind

Another element crucial to serving strategy is the wind. The wind can turn a weak serve into an ace and make a great serve untouchable. Many players, especially those new to the outdoor game, underestimate the wind's power to change a game. Even fewer actually know how to use the wind to their advantage. In fact, many players see wind as a nuisance. Good players use the wind and take advantage of players who do not understand the effects of the wind on the ball.

Several serves work against the wind. A common serve people use is the topspin serve. The wind will actually take a ball with spin on it and seem to push it down into the court. Another technique is lightly lofting a serve and letting the wind take the ball with it. In this situation, the wind does most of the work and can cause the ball to dive or change direction unexpectedly.

The single most important thing you must know is that on a windy day it can be more beneficial to you to choose the correct side than it is to choose whether to serve or receive. On days that are particularly windy, most of the points scored will occur only on one side of the court. This is not a coincidence. That side of the court is the one where the wind is blowing "against you," or at your face, as you are looking at the net. A good player will choose this side, because he or she has confidence in their ability to sideout. They will also have a huge serving advantage until it is time to switch sides.

It is a huge benefit to serve into the wind, especially if you are a good server. Here are a couple of scenarios. First, you serve a ball deep. On any other day, that ball would be out, but, with the wind pushing against it, the ball will land farther inside the court. This is hard for your opponents to pass because, until the last 10 feet of court, it appears as though the ball is going out of bounds. Meanwhile, when your opponents serve you can step back, as they are likely to serve deeper in the court—perhaps serving out long because the wind is with them. Another advantage is that even the most mediocre of float serves will become almost impossible to pass because the wind will make it hang or flutter in the air.

If your opponent does manage to pass the serve, the wind may blow the set over the net so that you can block it or make a play. Again, even if the set does stay on your opponent's side of the net, the hitter may have trouble tracking and timing a set that is moving around more than usual. I have seen great players look downright uncoordinated trying to hit on a windy day!

Now that you know the advantages, you have to learn to take advantage. If you have a choice of side on a windy day, then make the right choice. If you lose the toss and your opponent does not choose side, make sure you pick the side where the wind is against you. You should practice in windy conditions to get a sense of how the ball moves. Sometimes it is hard to make contact serving if the wind pushes your toss—especially high tosses—so you need to get a feel for that and how to adjust your toss in the wind.

Practice Makes More Perfect

Serving is the one skill you can practice completely by yourself. Practice all sorts of serves to all different spots on the court. Try out different types of serves and see over which ones you have the most command. At the same time, though, work on all your serves. You never know when you can use a particular serve to your advantage. Your opponents probably will not like adjusting to different types and speeds of serves coming at them during a game.

Also, start to view serving as your first chance to attack the ball. Let your serve set the stage for each play. Do not let your opponents off easy. Make them work the whole play to earn a point. If you place serving as a top priority in your preparation, you should start to see noticeable improvements in your results. You'll find you may start to challenge an opponent that regularly beat you previously, while you should be able to start beating close teams just by improving this aspect of your game. Remember, all top athletes possess confidence and aggressiveness; you should embrace those qualities in your game, as well.

4

It All Starts With a Pass!

You may be great at hitting the ball, but that means nothing if you can't pass. One thing that really elevates an Open level team above an "A" level team is the ability to pass the ball consistently. Bad passes lead to bad or loose sets and—even worse—potential instant points for your opponent.

Common Passing Mistakes Good <u>Indoor </u>Players Make <u>Outdoors</u>

Most players typically play doubles after the indoor season and quickly find they then face additional challenges. For starters, you have to cover more court because you only have two passers, as opposed to three or four. You also need to have more range, be more aggressive in going for balls and have great communication skills since a lot of balls will be served between you and your partner.

The good news is that a pass doesn't have to be perfect—as it does indoors—in order to run a good offense. In indoor sixes, the perfect pass is a little bit right of the middle of the court and no more than a foot off the net. In doubles, you can pass the ball almost straight in front of you and a little toward the middle of the court nearer your partner. The pass should be about five-to-eight feet off the net. This works in doubles because most players get lower sets that do not travel as far from the setter. The set has to be different in this way to account for wind and sun factors that players don't have to worry about indoors.

A common mistake that indoor players make is in their court positioning. Indoors, it is legal to open hand receive. Essentially, you push the ball to the setter with your hands apart, using your fingers to direct the ball to the target. In doubles, this type of play is illegal. Players are only allowed to pass the ball overhead—as long as their hands are together and the ball is not a lift, a double hit, or contacted with the player's fingers.

Not only is this hard to do, but this type of pass—even when well executed—rarely is good, especially for beginner and intermediate players. Despite this fact, far too many players still stand at the same place—about 15 feet from the net—whether they are playing indoors or outdoors. In doubles, if you stand that shallow you will usually get beat deep because you will not be able to cover behind you on the court.

Instead, because you can't open hand receive in the outdoor game, it is preferable to stand between 20-to-23 feet off the net until you can figure out where you are comfortable. This way, you will rarely get beat deep because those balls you might have felt tempted to play with your hands will most likely be out. You'll also still have time to move up for shorter serves and probably will find that a high percentage of serves you have to play in doubles usually land in the back half of the court.

It is a well-known fact that it is much easier to move forward for a ball than it is to move backward. Once you get comfortable, you might adjust where you stand. For example, if you notice your opponent is only serving short, you can move closer. You may also want to move up if the wind is blowing at your back, as your opponent's serves might drop shorter than usual. Whatever you do, your goal on serve receive should be to position yourself where you can cover the most ground and get to the highest percentage of serves.

Technique

There are some other things to think about when you pass. Even though I have spent some time talking about the adjustments you will need to make from the indoor game to the outdoor game in order to pass successfully, the same fundamentals do apply.

You still need to stay low, as opposed to standing up straight. Swinging your arms during passing should also be avoided because that makes for a higher, spinney pass—factors that make a ball harder to set. On harder serves you want to take the speed off the ball, pulling your arms into your body as you pass to absorb the ball with your whole body. You will notice that your passing platform will change because you do not need to guide the ball all the way to the net, but just to your partner, who will be moving as you pass. Doing these small, but crucial, things can make it easier for your partner to control the ball and get you an accurate set.

You should also avoid passing outside of your body, or reaching for the ball, as much as possible. In this case, a wet ball or hard serve would be more likely to fly off your arms, even though the outdoor ball is more forgiving than the indoor ball. Instead, your goal should be to use footwork to position yourself so that your shoulders and body are in front of the ball. This is not an easy task because you will face harder serves and have more space to cover. There will be times where you will have to rely on emergency tactics and reaching to steer the ball to your partner. However, the better and faster your footwork, the less you will have to resort to doing these things.

Tips and Strategies

Once you begin to feel comfortable serve receiving and producing good passes, you may want to consider some of these serve receive tips and strategies:

1. Watch The Server's Hand

Watch the ball as it leaves the server's hand. This will give you clues to the path of the ball and give you more time to react and the track the ball. You can tell the following:

    A. A ball will be topspin if the server's hand comes over the ball;

    B. A ball will be a floater if the server's hand stays behind the ball;

    C. A ball will be a cutter if the server's hand comes around the ball; and

    D. You will be able to determine if the serve is going to be short if the server's arm speed slows down or drops toward the end of the serving motion.

A common mistake that players make is only looking for the ball when it gets to the net. By doing this, a player only has about 20 feet of reaction space, as opposed to 50 feet.

2. Note your opponents' tendencies:

    A. Do they only serve deep? If so, stand deeper.

    B. Do they ever hit the line? If not, move in to play the percentages and challenge them to hit a spot they have little success hitting.

C. If they do have a good line serve, move to the line and force them to try to fit it in a smaller place, which could result in an error if they go for that serve. Chances are you will be taking their strength away as they will choose to serve elsewhere since you have "their" spot covered!

3. Challenge The Server

As you play more against a certain opponent, you will begin to learn the spots they like to serve, where they seldom serve, and where they make errors. If you know an opponent messes up when they try to serve short, stand back in the court and try to tempt them to serve short. It's a win-win situation for you because, they will either:

A. Serve it in the net trying to put it short;

B. Serve it to you easily because they want to go for the short spot but are afraid of making the error; or

C. Hit their spot. If they do manage to do this, it's still not a problem because you will be there to pass that serve since you baited them into it!

4. Taking Pressure Off Your Partner and Putting It On Your Opponent

Back to baiting! Since doubles is a game of survival of the fittest, if your partner is weaker than you or struggles passing, expect almost every serve to be aimed your partner's way. This can leave you feeling frustrated and your partner stressed. But, you can relieve this pressure and increase your opponents' frustration by shifting closer to your partner's side of the court.

This does two things:

a.   It leaves a lot of court open on your side and will make an opponent want to go for the empty spot. I have found that most players that fall for that bait will try to put a pretty decent serve to the empty spot. Usually they do not go after it with all they've got because they subconsciously know that they are playing right into your game. As long as you anticipate the server might go for the space you left, you should still be able to get back to your spot and pass the ball. Still, opponents who know you might move back may feel pressured to make the serve more difficult and place the serve so that it gets to the spot before you do. If they are not used to serving that way, they will most likely make an error. *Note: do not resort to this if the opponent's best serve is to the spot you are leaving open*!

b.   The second reason this tactic works is because many players will not fall for the bait. They will see right through what you are doing and will continue to serve your partner. Because of your shift, this is now okay. By moving more to the middle, you give your opponents a smaller window to hit if they wish to serve your partner. You will find your opponent may serve it easier to get it to your partner, or may serve it out trying to fit it into the smaller space. And, in a best-case scenario, you may actually wind up passing the ball if it drifts your way, thereby handling a ball that would have been your partner's if you hadn't moved. This relieves your partner and makes it easier for them to pass, which is usually the hardest skill to perform under stress. Even if your opponent still manages to serve hard at your partner, it will be trouble-free since you have eliminated the amount of court your partner has to cover, reducing their anxiety. In addition, you will begin to see your opponents get frustrated and impatient if you can use the shift effectively.

5. Neutralize Their Blocking—Passing for the "On-Two" Attack

If your opponent is blocking successfully and carelessly by setting up alongside the net and waiting for the targeted hitter, you need to keep your opponent honest. Start passing a little bit tighter than normal—maybe about three feet off the net so that instead of setting, you or your partner can take the ball over on two. This will cause the blocker to wait to see what the setter is going to do before getting into position, which could lead to a hurried block or more space for the hitter. If the person who is serving is the primary blocker, you and your partner should shorten or lower your passes and sets to make the server rush to the net to block. The blocker may not reach the net, leaving it open, or put up a shoddy block that the hitter can tool. Eventually, you will tire out your opponent by making them sprint 30 feet each time they serve.

If your opponents' strategy is serving short so that the passer cannot get a full approach for the hit, a team should consider the on-two offense. Instead of trying to pass to the normal spot and rush back to get an approach, the passer should put the pass on the net—like an indoor pass—and let their partner have the option to hit. Most of the time, even if the opponent does expect this, it can be hard to defend. It can also be frustrating, since now the stronger hitter is getting open swings without having to pass.

6. Communicate before the serve.

One main problem players new to the doubles game have is figuring out who is responsible for getting a serve that lands in the middle of the court. Maybe you have heard of the "husband and wife" ball? That is when the ball lands in between two people without either player calling the ball or going for it. To prevent this, before your opponent serves either you or your partner should say "my middle," or "my call." That player is responsible for calling out who will pass the ball by yelling either "mine," or "yours." They also will receive serves that land in the middle of the court. Deciding whose job this is for each play is easy. The passer who is standing on the opposite side of the court from the server makes the call as they will have a better angle on a ball that cuts through the middle of the court.

Passing in the Conditions

Even when you seem to have mastered the art of passing, you will still face challenges. A major factor you will have to adjust for outdoors that is not even a concern in the indoor game, are weather conditions.

There will be days it will be rainy, which will make the court slippery and muddy. There are days it will overly sunny. And probably the worst condition for any passer—windy. Here are some ideas and tips for each condition:

Rain

Players are the most tentative in wet conditions. A slippery surface is a huge neutralizer because in these conditions the best team does not always win. In rainy weather the ball gets heavy rather quickly. Therefore, an opponent is not going to serve as deep as normally, so you can move up a couple steps to put you in a better position to play the ball. This will prevent you from having to take extra steps toward the ball, which also means you will have less chance to slip.

When the ball is heavy due to wet conditions, sometimes you may have to deviate from normal passing form. A weighted down ball will not travel very far, so a good pass on a dry day is not going to make it to the same spot as on a wet day. You will need to give the ball an extra push and some extra height to make sure that your partner has enough time to get to the ball. That may mean you swing your arms ever so slightly when you pass. The ball won't shank off your arms as wildly when it is heavy. It is more important than ever in conditions like these to get in front of the ball. If you reach for the ball, your arms may not be strong enough to push a waterlogged ball to your target.

If you play on the grass, your footwork will also be slightly different on a wet day. When the ground is slippery, long and fast strides to the ball can result in slipping mid-play. Rather, take short and sure steps to get to the ball. You will have time, as the serve will not be traveling as fast. If you are a good passer, wet conditions should benefit you. Teams with the most ball control tend to win in these types of conditions, since they can adapt more readily.

Sun

A lot of players get caught up in the fact that they cannot see in sunny conditions. Yet, these tend to be the same players who are not wearing sunglasses. When I first started playing, I hated wearing sunglasses. I did not like the feeling of them on my face and I felt that they created some blind spots. It turns out that I was not wearing the right type.

Most people who have the same complaints also have never worn special athletic sunglasses. I strongly recommend that you invest in a pair. This investment is going to run around the neighborhood of $75 to $150. What you are looking for is a light pair of sunglasses with non-metal frames. You want the glasses to have a rubber nose piece and rubber pieces around the ends of the glasses to prevent them from slipping or moving during the course of play. The half jacket variety made by Oakley, which has no frame around the bottom part of the lens, restricts your vision the least. The best feature of the half jacket is that you can purchase different lenses to adjust for different degrees of light. If you buy a good pair of sunglasses you will eliminate most of your sun-related problems.

Sun usually is not a factor in passing because the sun is above your line of vision. However, some opponents may try to make you find the ball in the sun by utilizing a sky ball, which is an underhand serve that can go as high as 30-35 feet. Because the ball hangs in the air so long, it gives the passer more time to lose the ball in the sun. In some situations, the sun may only affect the left side player, so the right side player still has more than enough time to step in and pass the serve. But, this isn't an option if the sun is directly behind the server. Some players will still have a hard time passing the sky ball, even when they are in position. This is because the ball has so much spin on it as it drops that it sometimes moves away from you and curls back toward the net. To make passing the ball a little easier, take a step up as you are about to pass the ball, making sure that you have kept your shoulders and platform facing your target.

Wind

If you learn to make the wind an ally rather than an enemy, you will have great success. Adjust your positioning to account for the wind. For example, if the wind is blowing at you rather strongly, move back. The ball will carry deeper in the court than it normally would. If the wind is blowing away from you, you can expect a served ball to be shallower or drop. Whatever the situation, you should think about which way the wind is blowing. Then, consider the probable impact it will have on the path of the ball. Once you can recognize the wind and its' effect on the ball, you can put yourself in a better starting position to intercept the serve.

Final Thoughts

Make sure that you don't neglect the skill of passing. Serve receive is the one area of a player's game that can easily be exposed if it is thought to be a weakness. If you remember to position yourself effectively, account for your opponent's serving tendencies and take the weather conditions into account, you will solve half the battle. The rest comes from your ability to determine the path of the serve, your footwork getting to the ball and your intentness to pass the ball. Of course, to develop these areas, you will need experience and practice passing. So, keep playing!

5

Setting—The Course to Victory

Setting is one of the more difficult skills to master. Setters must have ball control, and be consistent. They must turn each pass, no matter where it is, into a consistently placed set. They must be able to take even a high, or spinney pass, and control it and account for wind conditions and adjust the set accordingly. The skill is a mix of technique, court smarts, chemistry with a partner and feel. And, those are reasons why not every one is a great setter.

If you want to play with better partners, become a better setter. Everyone loves to play with someone who can set him or her well. There are many things to think about if you wish to improve this part of your game and improving your control and consistency are the most important.

Bump Setting

This is the more popular style of setting. Many of the best players in the world choose to bump set because most players do not want to risk losing a point because of a "hands" call. Players that are not natural setters also may not be comfortable using their hands. Two great things about bump setting is that it will not result in a ball handling error, which could be a huge momentum changer; and a bump set can be used on any type of pass. Even Stein Metzger who was an All-American setter at UCLA and Misty May, an perennial All-American at Long Beach State, do not always hand set in tournaments.

Some believe that when you choose to bump set, you choose to sacrifice some accuracy and control. But, with practice, you can overcome this pitfall. Usually bad sets are a product of a lazy bump setter who is not focusing on the set. A common problem, resulting in a bad set, is swinging your arms at the ball to set it because control is sacrificed if a setter simply uses his or her arms to push the ball to the spot. Instead, a setter needs to make sure he or she gets to the ball and gets under it. A good setter also uses his or her arms to cushion the ball and take off any spin, and then uses his or her legs to push the ball to the spot the hitter wants it.

Using your legs, instead of your arms, to guide the ball helps a bump setter gain more control and consistency. Whenever you have executed a set poorly, you will find that you probably failed to do that very thing.

Hand Setting

Some players prefer a handset to get more control of the ball and to produce a more accurate set. Just as you would indoors, you want to get your feet to the ball and get under the ball. One main difference between hand setting indoors, versus outdoors, is that players use their fingers to push the ball indoors and use more of their hands on the outdoor ball. This is mainly due to differences in officiating.

Outdoor officials and organizations tend to judge sets by the amount of spin on the ball. At tournaments where there are no officials, playing teams are expected to work some of their off-matches. Since many of these players have little or no experience officiating, tournament directors do not trust in work teams to call doubles or carries consistently, or correctly. This is why there is a spin rule, which stipulates that any set that does not spin more than one and a half times is legal. Anything beyond one-and-a-half rotations instantly gets called. Therefore, any player—good or bad, setter or non-setter—can apply the criteria consistently.

Players who use the indoor style, contacting the ball with more of their fingers, tend to make the ball spin slightly on release. That set, even though no violation may have occurred, will instantly get called. This has actually led outdoor setters to hold the ball more and direct it to where they want. In indoor sixes, officials would call this a lift but, for the purposes of outdoor doubles, you can take advantage of this style to get more control of your sets. Again, you need to practice to get the feel of this and to become good.

Movement to the Ball

As soon as you have identified that you are not passing the ball, transition into setting. Begin to move up and, as you do, open up to (face) your partner. If the ball is served toward your partner's line, you may want to start to take steps toward your partner. The pass may wind up right in front of your partner, and probably will not wind up exactly in the middle of the court. If you see that your partner is passing a ball from the middle of the court as you transition out of serve receive, step out wider. This will account for a pass that may drift more toward your side of the court.

When you make contact with the ball, make sure you are no longer facing your partner. If you are square to your partner when you set, which beginning players tend to do, you will wind up setting the ball right to where your partner is standing. The ball will wind up off the net and your partner will not be able to get an approach. Instead, begin to square toward the net so that the set leads your partner.

The Big 3: Distance, Height and Tightness

The three differences in set preference among players is distance from the setter, height, and tightness to the net. It may sound obvious but the setter's job is to put the ball where the hitter will have the most success terminating the play. Depending on your partner, the set will differ. I've played with partners who like their set tight and inside, and others who preferred the set off and outside. There is no textbook set. In fact, I have played with all sorts of partners, each one wanting a different set. Believe it or not, I even had one partner who wanted to be set a 1-ball, like a middle hitter!

Usually, a player will want a set that is in between him or her and the setter. Indoors, a left-side hitter actually approaches from outside of the court to hit. Outdoors, the left side player does not perform the same type transition and approach. Most players begin their approach from where they pass the ball. Therefore, a good set will not travel past the hitting shoulder.

Determining set height can be tricky. The taller the person you play with, the higher they will probably like their set. This is because they can reach higher to contact the ball. Shorter players tend to like lower sets so that they have to approach quicker. It helps them maximize their jump.

On sand, the set needs to be much higher than it does when playing on grass. Due to the surface, players need more time to approach on sand and a higher set gives a player that time. Unfortunately, a higher set also gives the wind a chance to affect the set so it helps to not set too high. The other drawback of a high set is that it gives blockers a chance to set up.

A setter also needs to communicate with their partner about how tight the set should be. Some hitters are not comfortable hitting too close to the net. If the other team has a big block—penetrating your side—or are blocking effectively, it is a good idea to bring the set off the net to give the hitter more space with which to work.

However, some players, especially if they are tall, still like the ball very close to the net because they plan on going over or off the block. If the other team is not blocking, it can be very beneficial to push the set tight enough where your partner can crank it without following through into the net. Even if the ball sails over it might result in a point, as the other team may not be able to identify and cover it.

KYP

In his autobiography Magic Johnson, a former point guard for the Los Angeles Lakers, had a mantra, which he called KYP—Know Your Personnel (Johnson, 1993). Given that the setter is the "point guard" of the court, it is not a far stretch to apply this to volleyball conversation. For the sake of this topic, I would slightly refine this statement to, "Know Your Partner." It is important to be able to deliver a set, but is vital to know what type of set your partner wants in different situations. Again, communication is vital, as all players are slightly different—especially when it comes to the sets they like.

It is pretty obvious that most players ask their partners in warm-ups where the set should be located. During warm-ups there is no blocker, no defender, little movement on the part of the passer or setter, and rare poor passes. In the game, the set location will not be so cut and dry. A good setter will find out where his or her partner wants a set in these situations:

- When the pass is off the net;

- When there is a blocker;

- When the passer has passed from deep in the court and there is a question whether the hitter should be led;

- If the defender is on the ground after digging a ball; and

- If the hitter has passed the ball on the opposite side of the court from where they usually pass.

It is crucial to know that the same set will not work for every situation in a game. For example, a player might normally like a set low and inside but, when diving for a ball and coming up with a dig, that same low set will not give enough time for the hitter to get back up and get a good swing at it. There is nothing worse than making an amazing defensive play, then having to give a free ball to your opponent because the set was off. A great setter will be flexible and always make sure to deliver the set to a spot where the hitter feels most comfortable and can have the best chance to hit for a point.

Figuring all this out could take place in a pre-match conversation, or might happen on the fly through audibles in the middle of a game. As a setter, your job should be to find this information out from your partner so that you can execute it in a game. Likewise, you should communicate this information to your partner. The more you and your partner play, the decision about what type of set to give in a particular situation will become automatic.

The Setter's Other Jobs

The setter's job does not end with the set. It is very important that the setter communicate with the hitter, telling the hitter if there is a block and where is the open spot. If there is no block or the blocker drops off, you may yell out something like, "nobody," or, "kill it." This lets your partner know that they can swing away! If there is a block, then call out the spot away from the defender.

One important part of giving a call is making sure that both you and your partner are on the same page. This means that you know what every call means. Several years ago, I got into a huge fight with my mixed-doubles partner over a miscommunication. He called, "cross" as I was hitting and when I hit cross, I got blocked. I thought "cross" referred to the open alley where I could swing. He meant that cross was the open spot and assumed that I would roll over the blocker and place the ball there. It seems obvious to me now that he made the right call but, it is easy to see why we had a misunderstanding.

Here's another example: Just last summer, I had a partner yell, "swing cross!" I wound up hitting a roll shot it right to the defender, who was planted cross-court. My partner told me she was trying to help me hit around the block, since it was a tight set! The lesson here is making calls without prior communication creates confusion. To avoid the problem, make it clear to your partner that you are calling out the open spot; otherwise your call may be misinterpreted.

In fact, there are many types of calls that you can give your partner. "Cross" is a ball that travels across the court from the hitter. "Line" is a ball that travels straight in front of the hitter. For strong side players, cross is to the right and line is to the left. It is the opposite for the right side hitter.

Sometimes, you may call one of these directions and also indicate "high," or "deep." High means a shot that goes over the block. Deep means a shot that lands in the back part of the court. Obviously, a short ball lands closer to the net. A common term for a short ball is a "cut shot." This is a short shot around the block—although it can be executed on an empty net—where the hitter contacts the ball, following through with their hand facing away from their body. Whatever you do, make sure you call the shot early enough for the hitter to process it and react. The tricky part is not calling it so soon and loud that the defender has a chance to react to your call. After you call a shot, you should cover your partner in case the hit is blocked.

Creating and Recognizing Opportunities

In a game, there will be times where your primary duty is to set. It may be because you are the stronger hitter, or it could be because your partner is struggling. Sometimes, a struggling partner who is getting all of the serves feels more pressure, which can have an adverse effect on their game. I have heard a lot of players complain after a loss that there was nothing they could do, and that their partner got all the serves. A good player will find a way to take control of a game when it is not in their hands.

That happened in the 2004 Olympics, when Elaine Youngs rarely got served. Instead, teams opted to take a chance on her partner, the five-foot-six-inch Holly McPeak. That did not mean Youngs had to accept that she was not a part of the offense. The team tweaked its offense and incorporated Youngs as a hitter off second balls to keep its opponents off-balance. Taking it on two, instead of setting, is an effective way to gain control of the game and counter the opponent's strategy. I am not recommending that all teams adopt the McPeak-Youngs offense. However, if a team thinks it can plant a blocker at the net, consider taking it on two a few times to keep your opponent honest. That way, they can't set up where they want to block.

As a setter you need to know how to give your hitter the best chance to put the ball away. Sometimes, if there is no block, you must push the set tighter than normal. Getting the hitter closer increases his or her chance of putting the ball away. As I said earlier, with no blocker, a tight set is no risk because, if it travels over the net, there will not be an opponent at that spot. Just make sure you are square, if you handset.

Another time you should try to push your set tight is on a bad pass. On a pass that is off the net teams will pull the block, not expecting the offense to mount a serious attack. If you become good at taking a bad pass and pushing it to the net, you will create both a higher percentage hitting opportunity for your partner and the mental lift of overcoming a near mistake. It also can kill the spirit of your opponents, as they may be expecting an easy point to be generated by the bad pass. Of course, you should talk this over with your partner so that he or she is prepared to get to the net on a bad pass.

Final Thoughts

The most important thing a setter can bring to the game is consistency. That is what separates a good player from a great player. If you want to play with great partners, become a great setter. It makes no difference whether you bump set or handset; the goal is to be able to put the ball in the spot where your partner wants the ball each and every time, even though the location of the pass may vary.

It is true that using your hands tends to result in a more consistent set, but you must first do what is comfortable. The only drawback to using your hands is that you risk getting called for a ball handling error, such as a double or a lift. However, the reward of accuracy can be worth the risk if you can perfect the skill. Like anything else, you have to practice to get a feel for things such as setting in the wind, setting from different spots of the court, etc.

6

Be a Terminator

Hitting is the most glamorized skill in volleyball. That is because it is the most flashy and powerful skill that exists in the game. To end a play successfully, your opponent has to make an error, or your partner and you need to produce a kill. At the higher levels, opponent errors are more rare and the ability to sideout relies on the strength of your offense, which is your hitting.

Most players identify two styles of hitters. The more popular style is the "jump high and smack it down" approach. This style can make a player readable because, if you hit as hard as you can, the hit usually goes where the arm and shoulders are facing. It can also result in more hitting errors. Yet, it is important to be able to develop this power in order to intimidate your opponent and challenge them on defense.

The second type of hitter is one who has a great command or control of his or her hits. That hitter may not pack a big wallop, but they can place the ball anywhere they want and are pretty consistent about keeping the ball in play. It also frustrates opponents, who do not understand why they cannot dig such an "easy" ball. The downside is that these shots may be able to be tracked down better than a ball that has pace on it against quicker opponents and better defenders. As time goes on, opponents will get used to the player's shots and get a better read on them, reducing the effectiveness.

The best hitters I have seen combine both elements of power and placement, making them unpredictable and virtually "un-diggable" to the opposing team. A player like this presents huge problems for an opponent. There are many components to hitting effectively that will be discussed here, including fundamentals, shot selection and strategy, as well as hitting around the block. If you can take something out of this and refine your game, offensively you could become almost unstoppable.

Fundamentals

As in passing, there are some adjustments that you will have to make from the indoor game to the outdoor game. The best thing about doubles is that if you make a good pass, you—not another teammate—will be the one rewarded with a set. So, to accomplish this, you must transition into your approach as soon as you pass the ball.

Unlike indoors, you are not going to get outside of the court to approach, or start your approach from a standard spot. You are going to start your approach from wherever you pass the ball from. This means that you will be getting a set and hitting farther inside of the court than usual. Taking the time to get outside of the court to hit a "four" ball is a waste of time and energy and can lead to an awkward "in and out" approach that will leave you off-balance. Instead, most sets should be between where you passed the ball from and the setter's position.

After you pass, you will take a step to get into position and then approach. Your steps will still be deliberate and powerful. You will still be generating a lot of power from your quads and arm swing (See Chapter 8 for tips on maximizing your vertical jump). On harder surfaces like grass, your approach will be made up of long steps. On sand, you will take shorter steps and jump straight up, rather than broad jump.

A huge misconception people have is that you have to hit the ball hard to be a great hitter. Unlike indoor, you will not have to get your ball past two blockers and four additional defenders. You just have to keep two players from digging you. It does not matter if you crush the ball, or roll the ball. All that matters is that you put it where the defenders are not.

You also may elect to have your partner call out a place on the court to hit if he or she sees an open spot. If there is a block, the call refers to the area that the block is leaving open. If you swing hard into that area, you will most likely get blocked, as that is the area the blocker is trying to take away with his or her hands. You may still swing hard, but, if you do, make sure there aren't any hands directly in the plane you are swinging over—or you will get "roofed" hard!

Going Down Swinging

Some players want to drill the ball every time they hit. Those are the same players who turn their noses up and curse when their opponents win by barraging them with roll shot after roll shot. They walk off the court and swear they will not play doubles again, ranting about how they cannot believe they lost to team that never hits the ball and does not play volleyball the "right way."

In reality, there is no one "right way" to play—and win—volleyball. The only "right way" is the way a team uses that helps them to win. And, for each team, that way may be different. I have seen players get upset and lose games because they were not ready for the unorthodox playing style of their opponents. Many of you probably have seen this happen to someone else, or have, at some point, experienced yourself. I have witnessed it several times over the years, and each time it makes me laugh because I used to be one of those uneducated players who did not understand the nuances of an effective doubles' offense.

It's not that you absolutely cannot win swinging as hard as you can on every set. However, you risk becoming predictable and not as successful if you don't mix in some off speed stuff or placement shots. The better your competition, the more true that statement becomes. If I had my way, I would try to crush the ball straight down every time I hit. But, that type of hitting invites a block, might reduce the amount of serves I see and will tire out my shoulder. And then, when my opponent does dig me, they will get the satisfaction and mental lift that digging a roll shot will not give them. This could turn the momentum of the game around.

Perhaps I am exaggerating as I try to detail the worst-case scenarios, but it should be pointed out that, eventually, opponents will lock in on your arm swing and read where you are hitting. The biggest problem with the "all or nothing" approach to hitting is if the set is off—due to wind, a bad pass, or because the ball gets heavy because of rain—you are going to have a hard time keeping up that style of hitting.

I know that despite reading what I just wrote, many of you still plan on going with this approach. That is fine, you can still be successful, but there are a couple of things to keep in mind during the course of a game that will make a difference in the outcome of your day. If you are a player who puts the ball away every time you are set, you can skip this part and move to the next section. Otherwise, all you "heavy hitters" out there should read on.

The first thing to keep in mind is the truth in the old saying, "if it ain't broke, don't fix it." If your team approach is scoring points for you, stick with it until your opponent adjusts and can shut you down consistently. If you are swinging as hard as you can and no one can dig you, keep swinging—regardless of whether the ball finds the court cleanly or shanks off one of your opponent's body parts.

I had a partner who was a great hitter but, whenever a team blocked, she stopped hitting and started rolling. Since she was not used to doing this, she was tentative and not as effective. What she had essentially done was take herself out of her own element by giving the defense respect that it had not yet earned. My partner later became much more successful once she committed to hitting and doing what she was used to doing in that situation. The only time she would consider changing her hitting style was if she got blocked, or dug. And, that is the only time you need to stop to think.

At the point when your opponent does stop you, ask yourself some questions. Did that dig happen because you hit it right at the person? Perhaps you might have gotten such a good set that you knew you were drilling it right at your opponent, but you were so pumped up to hit you did not care what was in your way. If this is the case, you may need to change your attitude. You might be overly greedy and, worse, you are showing that you do not respect the other team.

Taking things for granted and underestimating an opponent is a huge mistake. Most players who have a ball hit right at them will dig the ball, no matter how fast it is coming to them, or how bad they are. Once they make the dig, you will lose one big advantage you may have had before—intimidation! The other team now has confidence that it can dig you and it will be more zealous when you next attack!

Instead, consider a change of contact. For instance, if you notice that your opponent is right in the lane where you plan on slamming the ball, cut your hand around the ball or finish the swing across your body to make it travel in a different path. Your opponent will not be able to react to this sudden change in direction, and you will still have hit the ball hard. Remember, a winner is out to take each point, not to look good!

Another question you should consider is was the dig a fluke defensive play—like a one-handed up, or a ball that bounced perfectly off their shoulder? If the answer is "yes," do not change a thing. Challenge the defenders to make the same great play again. If the answer is "no," then you should be prepared for your opponents to start digging you more often because they figured out something. If this is the case, you need to start mixing it up to keep your opponent off balance. To help you do that, here are a few more offensive tools to add to your arsenal so that you will be less predictable.

Selecting your Shots

People tend to think that shots mean slow hits. This is hardly the case. Each shot has different cuts and speeds. To be effective on offense, a player should have a nice mix of control, placement and power.

It really doesn't take talent to hit the ball hard. The talent, and great skill, comes when you hit the ball hard to a given spot. Every great player should have the following attack options:

1.   Hard hits to the line, middle and cross court;

2.   Deep rolls to those areas; and

3.   Some sort of short ball, such as a cut.

The best players disguise their shots, taking the same approach every time and contacting the ball at the same point. To practice, I suggest the same sort of set up as you would to practice serving. Identify the shots you want to work on, hit several balls to each spot and try to get a feel for each type of hit. You can work with someone, who can set you, or you can toss the ball as you approach.

It is always good to mix up things. If all you do is hit hard, you will, likely, have your opponents playing deeper and more on their heels. This leaves the court open for a short roll shot. Other players swing cross most of the game. The opponent, knowing this, will shift more to that side of the court. By doing this, the hitter has shrunk the court because now the defender knows the hitter can't reach about five feet of court in the hitting zone. Now, if this player turned the ball line occasionally, he or she would have a wide-open shot. It would also keep the opponent honest and force the person into a more neutral defensive position. As you attempt to execute these different shots, do not drop your hitting shoulder. That motion will tip the defense off to the roll shot.

It is important that every great player be able to execute deep shots. At the higher levels of playing, blocking is a huge part of the game, a major part of a team's offense and an integral part of a team's defensive strategy. Most of the time, blockers at the Open level do take away the area they call and they also penetrate the net so that it is less likely they get "tooled." If a player swings away against a block like this, he or she is likely to get blocked. Even if they avoid the block, they will be hitting right at the defender. To avoid this, professional players increasingly are starting to use high roll shots over the block and away from the defender, only relying on the hard hit if they see it open. Again, if a player drops his or hitting shoulder, it will be difficult to get the shot over the blocker.

Around the Block

No one wants to give a good player an open look at the court. Many teams mainly block to take away a favorite hit, or to steer a hit toward a defender. Another reason teams block is to discourage the opponent from setting tight to the net. If the hitter chooses to hit their favorite shot, it will have to be altered. This may lead to a hitting error.

Some players enjoy the challenge of hitting past the block, while other players are intimidated. The latter are usually not successful.

The simple fact is if one of your two opponents is at the net, there is more court to hit. To maximize your performance in the presence of a block, you must possess a few things:

1. Court vision, or a partner who you trust to communicate open shots;

2. Control; and

3. Determination.

When I enter an Open tournament, I know most teams are going to block consistently as part of their game plan. There has been many times where I have played against blockers who were more than eight inches taller. On paper, you wouldn't expect me to do well in that situation, but I have been able to neutralize big blocks and win tournaments thanks to great communication on the part of my partner, and my ability to execute the shots that are called. If you practice the three "musts" I mentioned above, you can overcome blocking mismatches, where you are the underdog.

Before any match you need to prepare in order to be successful. If you have played a team before, you know their tendencies. If you have never seen a team play, you need to spend time watching the day of the tournament. What you should look for is the team's blocking trends and the defender's skill. In particular, look for the areas that the blocker seems most comfortable taking away.

Here are some questions to ask yourself as you watch:

1. Do they like blocking line or cross better?

2. Does the blocker actually take away what the signal says?

3. Do they penetrate the net?

4. Do they play tricks and shift their block mid-approach?

5. Does the defender just play the area the blocker leaves? If so, you can roll shot to the empty area every time.

6. Does the defender wait in the middle to try to intercept the setter's calls?

7. Is the defender quick? The quicker the defender, the more likely your roll shots will be run down, so you will have to put some more pace and less arc on them.

8. Does the defender try to push the ball back over the net instead of pass it? Then, any sort of roll shot made in front of the defender will be playing right into their strategy. As "cheesy" as people might think it is, some defenses operate this way. It must be considered when game planning, because there are teams that use the "over on one" to score points rather effectively.

Try to consider all of the above when coming up with your game plan. This way you will know how you will attack the game when confronted with a block. Again, the goal is to play the game using your team's strengths while exploiting your opponents' weaknesses!

When it comes time to play the game, you have to enter with the mindset to be aggressive. Recognize your opponent's block, but, until and unless it becomes effective, you do not have to let it dictate how you play. That means that you will not change your approach or alter your game until your opponent forces you to do so.

Until you have gotten blocked or gotten dug due to the block, there is no reason to change a thing. Too often, players just assume they have to do roll shots to avoid the block. I encourage players to swing hard around it, if the option is there, and see if the defender behind the block is worthy. Once you get blocked or dug—and it will happen no matter how much you don't want it to—you must make adjustments. That's when it will come in handy to have control of a variety of shots.

Trouble Sets

Another reason that you cannot swing as hard as you can all of the time is because the set may not always be there. Even if your partner is a great setter, sometimes you may have to hit a bad set. It might be due to a bad pass, wind, or just poor execution.

If the set is off the net you can still swing hard but, as you reach behind you, you will probably strain your back. Instead, you should learn to adjust your approach for this type of set. Most opponents will expect you to hit deeper when you are off the net, so don't be afraid to risk a short shot. They will also expect your shot to land in the middle of the court assuming that you do not want to make an error. Knowing that, feel free to direct your hit toward a sideline, as your opponent may instinctually be moving in to the middle. Realize that if your opponent sees your shoulder drop, they will catch on to what you are doing. This is why it is important to stay behind the ball so that you can conceal your shots.

If the set is too tight, you need to hit without going into the net. If you take a full swing, it will be hard to avoid contact with the net. In doubles, it is not legal to open hand tip, or direct the ball with your fingers. This makes dealing with a tight set even more challenging.

Instead, close your hand into a fist and poke the ball over the net. If you watch how your opponent reacts to this, you can poke it short or deep to keep it away from your opponent. You can also follow through with your fist to the left or right, as most opponents will expect a "poked" ball to travel in line with the hitter either short or deep. If you change the direction, you may through them off further.

The worst-case scenario is a set that drifts over the net to your opponents' side. Be ready to transition from hitter to blocker. If you opponent tries to attack your set, get your hands up and try to push the ball back into their court.

Winning Warm Ups

A team earns no points by "winning warm-ups." A lot of players will use warm ups to try to look good and take swings they might not take in the game. Use hitting time wisely and what it is meant for—warming up.

Get a feel for the ball and work on your shots. Really focus on the fundamentals. Also, remember that it is a warm-up. I have seen players take 10-15 hits. Not only does this tick off your opponent, but it will only tire you out, let your opponent see more things about your offensive style and give them practice reading your arm swing.

Limit your swings. Practice a roll shot to the line, middle and deep cross. Then, take a short cut shot. Make your last three swings a hard hit line, one to the middle, and one cross-court. If you miss one of these and want to take another one, go for it. If your opponent sees all of these different hits, they will have to respect your offense. More importantly, they will not be able to start off the game cheating because you will have shown them many looks.

I have found that you can usually warm up fully with ten or less hits, but I have seen great players take only three or four. Do what you need to do to go into the game feeling prepared, but also remember to "save some for the game."

Final Thoughts

Find a balance. Many people define a player based on his or her hitting skills. Therefore, do not become one-dimensional. Do not rely on hard hits and a high jump to carry you through a tournament or a playing career. Gradually, practice different shots and incorporate them into your game. If you mount a balanced attack, it will not be easy for your opponents to play defense. There will come a day when you will not be able to swing as hard or jump as high, and when that happens you will be thankful that you worked on all aspects of offense because you will be able to remain competitive.

7

Nothing Hits Defense

Defense is an attitude, but not every player is defensive-minded. That's because most people admire the flashiness of hitting and it also seems to be the skill that more players try to hone. If you want to win, though, especially at the higher levels, you need to start to take as much pride in your defense as you do in your offense.

The best defense players use their heart and their head. Playing great defense requires you to read the hitter, but also to want to dig the ball and do whatever it takes to keep the ball off the ground. As great as that philosophy sounds, simply wanting to dig the ball is not going to result in a dig—although it never hurt anyone's chances! But, generally, you simply need to do other things to tilt the game in your advantage.

Playing with Your Head and Your Heart

Defense starts with positioning. Trying to cover half the court and perhaps more if your partner is blocking, can be a daunting task, especially if you don't play the percentages. If you don't know anything about your opponent, it is best to stay in a neutral position. Play a couple feet off your line and about mid-court, until you see what the hitter can do. This will allow you to get short balls and you will still be able to use your hands to dig deep shots. As you get to know your opponents, you might realize they rarely, if ever, hit deep. That means you can move up in the court because that is where the highest percentage of hits will land.

Readiness is also important. Your weight needs to be on the balls of your feet. You should never be planted, or you will not be able to adjust to an off-speed roll shot. You arms should also be in neutral position so, if necessary, you can adjust to a high hit and take it over your head. When playing defense, find the hitter. Stay still once they contact the ball, which allows you to react faster to the hit.

You also need to read the set. If the set is off the net, your opponent will not be able to hit down, or shallow, in the court unless they use a roll shot. This means you can move back for a harder hit, but that you also will still be ready for an off-speed shot.

Some sets dictate that a certain hit will be coming. If the set is very tight to the net to the point where the set is in the plane, some hitters may poke the ball to avoid contact with the net. So, watching the set is important in figuring out how you should be positioned.

However, you still need to pay attention to other aspects of the game because, against a great player or team, knowing tendencies might help, but not much. When the set is perfect and in the hitter's wheelhouse, the hitter should be able to hit virtually anywhere and at any speed.

Reading the hitter, not simply guessing, is another valuable skill to have. Falling into the "guessing game" is a common mistake. Instead of watching the hitter, some players guess where the ball might go, based on what the hitter last hit or likes to hit. Although anticipation can be useful, it should not be the cornerstone of your defense. Great players rely on the "clues" a hitter gives them.

Here are some things to look for:

The Hitter's Shoulders—Looking at the way the hitter's shoulders are facing can give you a good idea of where the hitter is aiming. If the hitter's shoulders are square to the line, that is most likely where the hit will land, unless the hitter cuts the ball or swings away from his or her body.

The Hitter's Hand—If the hitter's hand is closed, the shot will go in one direction, either deep or short. It will only vary if the hitter follows through and knocks his or her fist when contacting the ball. However, few players do that since poking is more of an emergency tactic used to reach a tight set, rather than a planned attack. As soon as a team identifies that the poke is being used, the defender in front of the hitter needs to cover the short poke. A good teammate, instinctively, should cover the area behind his or her partner to take the deep ball.

The Hitter's Arm—Most great players try to disguise their roll shot. Not all are successful and some give off "tells" about the type of hit they will execute. If you see a player's hitting arm drop or their approach slow down that is a clear sign that a roll shot is coming, so, do not plant!

The Hitter's Approach—Watching the path the hitter takes to the ball can tip you off to where the hit might go. If the hitter has to travel far in the court to reach the set, he or she may not have the time, or be able to stop their momentum, and he or she will have no choice but to hit in the direction that they are approaching.

If the hitter overruns the ball and catches it behind them, the hit will be deeper than usual, unless the hitter chooses to roll. You will also have cases where the hitter does not quite get to the set and has to hit outside his or her body. In this case, the ball will travel in the same direction as the hitter's arm—away from the body.

Another clue is the speed of the approach. The faster the approach, the harder the hit will be, since the hitter has more momentum. If you see a hitter take small stutter steps to the ball, that is a sign that the hitter may plan to try an-off speed shot.

The Hitter's Eyes—There will be times the hitter will look to see where the defenders are, especially with a block up. In my experience, if a hitter has locked eyes with me, they have never hit it at me! Knowing this, if you make eye contact with the hitter, sprint to the empty spot just as soon as the hitter's eyes leave you to find the ball. You can come up with a lot of digs this way. Watching the hitter's eyes, like a cornerback watches a quarterback's eyes, will allow you to get a jump start to where the ball is going and to pick off the ball.

If you can try to focus on a couple of these signs that hitter's give off, you should find yourself making more digs. Granted, you can't look for all of these things every time, but being aware of them can help you react and make some good choices at key moments in the game.

Attitude

Another thing to remember is that the player that wants the ball gets the ball. You will not dig the ball if you do not try for it. Sometimes, players give up on the ball because, for some reason, they do not think they can get to it.

You should never think that way. Every great defensive player has the mindset and the determination that the ball will NEVER hit the ground. Indeed, there will be times where you might not make a great dig but, because you simply played a ball and kept it in play, the pressure is put back on your opponents. If you do not come up with the ball, you are not worse off for trying. If you do come up with the ball, your opponent may make a mistake. At best, you might even be able to produce a kill.

In doubles, when you get a defensive touch on the ball you are creating an opportunity for your team to score a point that you would not have normally had, especially with the rally format where every point counts. Making a play like this could turn the game around in your favor. So, the next time someone rolls short, run it out. Most players have a lot more range than they realize. You just may surprise yourself.

Blocking Fundamentals and Strategies

At the upper levels, blocking is a major part of a team's defensive strategy. In the AA and Open levels, it is never a good idea to let high-caliber players hit on an open net. Great players will put the ball away almost every time they are put in that situation.

To be an effective blocker you do not always have to block the ball back into your opponent's side of the court. You can also alter the opponent's shot and take away part of the court. Most players can be effective blockers if they can reach their hands completely over the net. There are times where Misty May, who is only five-feet, nine-inches, blocks, instead of her partner Kerri Walsh, who is six-feet, three-inches. Even though May is not tall by beach standards, she gets high enough above the net to prevent her opponents from hitting straight down. If she is playing an opponent who likes to hit line, she can prevent them from hitting hard line and make it so that the only way the ball can be hit down the line is if it is hit over her block.

To do this, her opponents have to alter their hit to go over her block, which means they will have to hit it higher. Therefore, the ball will travel slower, giving May's partner enough time to be able to get to the ball. If the hitter decides to hit it around May's block they will hit cross, which is where Walsh would be standing.

It seems simple enough. May and Walsh make it look easy on a regular basis, but there are a lot of things that go on behind the successful execution of this defensive scheme. The reason I used this example was to stress the point that you do not have to be tall to be a successful blocker, even at the highest level of play.

While you don't, necessarily, have to be tall to be a good blocker, you do have to be a good decision-maker. Not all teams know when to block and, truthfully, blocking is not a necessity for all teams. At lower levels where hitters are not as effective it is not worth blocking and it is better to have two defenders covering the court. It is only necessary to block if the set is continually coming over the net or a hitter is consistently putting away the ball and it can't be stopped by the defense. In most cases, that team will serve the other partner.

At the higher levels, both partners will be capable of siding out consistently. Like any sport, it is never good to let an opponent get comfortable. If a hitter is in the groove, the defense has to get the hitter out of that comfort zone. Blocking can be a constant part of the game, or can be used sporadically, depending on who is served and the type of set.

However, it is not just about getting the block, because high-level players will not hit into a single block more than once or twice a game. Usually, it is because the set is too tight. Therefore, as a blocker, your goal should be to seal off an area. At the start of the game most blockers try to seal off the side they are playing, so that their partner can stay on his or her own side. As the game goes on, adjustments are made.

Speaking from a strategy standpoint, it is always best to block your opponent's favorite shot, or hardest hit. If you notice a player loves to crank the ball down the line, then that is the area you should block. To set up, position yourself right in front of the hitter and jump as high as you can, making sure your hands are turned into the court. Your opponent is not going to be able to crush it down the line because your hands will be in the way. So, they will either have to hit somewhere else or will have to roll it over your block.

If they do choose to hit, they will have to hit around you cross-court, which is where your partner will be positioned. The best-case scenario is that they will hit it right into your hands. It can be incredibly frustrating over time for your opponent if they cannot hit their spot, or hit it as hard as they want. And, it is even more frustrating if the blocker actually blocks the hit. As the game goes on, if the hitter gets comfortable rolling over you or hitting around you, move your block to mix it up.

Blockers can also trick their opponents into hitting a spot. For example, you set up like you are blocking line. Then, as the hitter is approaching, you do a quick shuffle step and move your hands to block the cross-court hit—completely surprising the hitter.

I have also played some mind games with opponents who have shown tendencies in the presence of the block. I play one opponent who likes to roll the ball short when a block is put up. Sometimes, what I like to do is signal to my opponent that I am blocking line and tell them to play for the short crosscourt hit, or cut shot. As the hitter approaches, I wait for the player to recognize that I am blocking and I drop off quickly toward the line. The result is either my partner or I usually come up with the ball and usually converts the dig into a point for our team. Communication is a key here so you must tell your teammate what you are doing for this to work. This sort of play will not work every time, but it is something a team may want to try occasionally. Either way, learning a hitter's tendencies will help you arrange successful defensive schemes.

Setting Up a Blocking Scheme

Several things need to happen in order for a team to use the blocking strategy to its' advantage. One key part of blocking is communication. Before your team serves, you must call your defensive coverage, or how you will defend each hitter. The standard way to do this is through blocking signals. The player nearer the net uses his or her hands and fingers to signal the coverage. That person is not always the blocker, but calls the game with their hands behind their back so the opponent cannot see the game plan. The number of fingers they hold up on their right hand refers to how the team will play the player to its' right (the strong side player). In the same way, the left hand signals how the team will play the opponent on its' left (the weak side player).

The number of fingers held out signals the coverage. One finger means the blocker should take the line, two means cross, and all five fingers showing means that the blocker is going for the ball. A closed fist indicates that the blocker will either be pulling off the net or not blocking at all. In some cases, when holding these signals on both hands the caller will move or shake one of their hands to show the server which player to serve.

If, for some reason, the blocker is going to change strategy and coverage, he or she will have to put his or her fist behind his or her back as they run to the net, holding the signal so the defensive player can see the signal. If the blocker cannot do this, the digger will have to read where the blocker sets up on the hitter. At the same time, the blocker should try to reach as high as possible to create an obstacle for the hitter. The best blockers penetrate into the opponent's court. If the ball gets past the block, the blocker should turn from the net and find the ball so that they can be in position to make a good set, if their teammate comes up with a dig.

Before the serve, the blocker should be no more than 10 feet off the net and positioned in the center of the court. If a blocker stands more to one side, it may tip off where the serve is going. You never want to give away your strategy, even if you feel it is obvious, as it can be more calming for an opponent to pass when they know you are specifically serving them. Sometimes this motion will put more pressure on the passer. However, it is always best in doubles to stay in a neutral position, in case your opponent overpasses the ball or has to take it on two.

The server usually is the defender, although some teams use the same blocker the whole game. Whatever the case, the defender should be positioned behind the block as the serve goes over the net. This helps hide the defense. The hitter will have to guess the defender's position. This also gives the defender a chance to pick up on the setter's call and adjust. You should always avoid letting your opponent see where you plan to play defense. Each time the opponent gets the ball, you should transition into this type of formation. Hide your digging assignment as much as possible!

Having said that, there are some cases where you may actually let the opponent see your coverage. For example, if your teammate is blocking line, let the hitter see you cross-court. If they see you, instantly sprint to the line for the deep roll.

Sometimes, it may be beneficial to mix the two styles. For example, hide behind the block and fake like you are moving to the line. Doing this may get the setter to call out, "cross" as the empty spot. As soon as you juke line and if you intercept the call, reverse your step and spring cross. More often than not, you will come up with the dig. Used correctly, these plans can work masterfully. They key is to continue watching the hitter so you can make educated decisions about where to move on the court. It is still important to mix up these strategies, however, because, if an opponent knows your moves, they will no longer fall for them.

Pulling off vs. Staying on the Net

There will be times the blocker will have to make adjustments. For example, if the set is bad, the hitter will not be effective. If the set is off the net, the hitter will not be able to get a good swing at the ball, so the blocker should drop quickly off the net into the area where they were supposed to block. If for some reason the blocker cannot make a quick drop, he or she should back up with their hands up and prepare to dig overhead. On the other hand, if the set is incredibly tight, the blocker should abandon his or her strategy and go for the ball.

Final Thoughts

Some people are naturals at defense and can read their opponents like a book. For those of you who do not have this natural talent, try to pick up on the "tells" given to you by your opponent. Do not make defense a guessing game. The best way to do this is to play as much as possible so you can get more experience reading the hitter. Eventually, you will naturally react to situations.

If you have a net and a partner to practice with, work on digging balls to your left, right, in front of you and at your head. It will help you develop the confidence that you can handle these balls.

8

Let's Get Physical

No matter how good your skills, you will see your performance plummet throughout the day if you are not prepared for the physical nature of a tournament. The reasons could be as varied as fatigue, or a pulled muscle. Many times, I have seen players slow down at the end of a grueling tournament. They have not been conditioned to sustain their effort throughout the course of a day.

At the start of the day, they are jumping high. By the end of the day, their vertical and power decreased. The worst thing is seeing a team lose a game, or have to forfeit, because a player cramped and could no longer play. I am sure at some point you have all seen this happen to someone else, or experienced it yourself. To avoid this, it is just as important to get yourself physically ready to play as it is having the skills and mindset to play. If you are panting for breath, you will not be able to play your best. Having the skills is just the beginning. Having athleticism and strength enhances your fundamentals.

As you become a better player and start winning, certain teams will make beating your team their goal. Everyone plays harder against number one! That means that a committed team will work harder in preparation for your team. You may not be able to control whether a team outplays you, but do not let a team outwork you! And, never leave the court knowing that you could have done better. If you do not work to your potential, you are cheating yourself.

This doesn't mean that you have to have a Charles Atlas body, or that you have to run the 40-yard dash in four seconds. Have you ever seen a successful volleyball player jacked up? You probably have not for a variety of reasons. In doubles, you have to be well rounded skill-wise and physically. You need a good combination of balance, core strength, flexibility, quickness, stamina and jumping ability—especially if you do not have height.

A good athlete makes sure that all of these are addressed to some extent in their workout regimen. A person who is naturally a high jumper may not need to work on increasing his or her vertical. While it is always good to improve, that player may need to work more on conditioning, so that he or she can continue to jump to the same height throughout the course of a tournament. Another person may need to work on their ball-handling skills, rather than their physical conditioning.

No two athletes are the same, so a workout regimen that works for one may not address the needs of another. Therefore, there really is no "one size fits all" master plan. The key is to do what works for you and mix it up as needed. The purpose of you committing to a workout regimen is to tone and condition muscles you will use the most in a game, as well as to perform movements you would in a game.

In the next section, I will share some ideas concerning how to approach each area of training as well as give some sample exercises and workouts. From there, you should identify what areas you need to build on and what areas you need to sustain. Use this information to craft a regimen that best suits your current needs.

Strength

Some base strength is at the core of anything that you do. Before you even consider jump training, you need to build up muscles so that you don't injure yourself. Not everyone knows what exactly to lift, or how much and how many times. The problem is that different people will tell you different things. There are so many "experts," books, and online articles that discuss different philosophies of training. It is overwhelming when you consider all the research available.

The most important thing to remember is the best workout is the one that is right for you—even if it is not considered "textbook." Deciding what works best is a process. I have been involved in strength training for more than ten years and not a year has passed where I have not tweaked my workouts, either to meet my individual needs, or because of new research.

Your primary goal is to develop core strength. You do not have to have big, bulging biceps. Instead, look to tone the muscles you will be using in the game so, by the end of a tournament, those muscles are not fatigued to the point where your game suffers. Besides, it is rare to see people with huge muscles play volleyball, as those people tend to have less flexibility and agility and usually can not master all of the skills.

Your workouts should also be centered on body parts. Most lifters love to work their chest and biceps because those muscles show the most growth. I call these "the glamour muscles," because they might make a player look good and strong. But, the truth is developing those areas is the least important for volleyball players.

The upper body muscles used in volleyball primarily are the shoulders, back, forearms and triceps. Therefore, those are the areas of most concern. However, you cannot neglect opposing muscle groups, such as the chest and biceps, because they stabilize the back and triceps, respectively, but they will not be your central focus.

Your main emphasis should be your quads for lower body workouts. For passing and defense, you need to stay low. Your quads supply most of your power for jumping and, since your hamstrings work opposite to the quads, you also need to work on those. If you only work on building your quads and ignore the hamstrings, you will be more likely to pull a muscle, due to muscle imbalance. You will also use your calves for jumping and your gluteus muscles on defense. Of course, you also need to lightly hit on the muscles stabilizing the legs, such as your hip and thigh abductors.

How much weight you lift will change as you spend more time in the gym. It also depends on the time of the year. During the off-season, you will most likely be trying to build strength. As the season approaches, you switch your emphasis to stamina. Your goal should be to do three sets of ten to twelve repetitions for each exercise. Use enough weight so that you feel your muscles working on the seventh and eighth repetition. By the time you get to the last repetition, your muscles should be tired to the point where you can't do another repetition. If you can do at least fifteen repetitions without a sweat or struggle, you should increase the weight.

During the off-season, you should have a pretty aggressive approach to weight training and try to get to the gym at least five days a week. And, ladies, you will not become "the Incredible Hulk" if you lift this way.

Way too many women use the, "I don't want to get big" excuse as a cop-out for why they do not weight train. This is one of the biggest perpetuated misconceptions out there. It is a simple fact that women do not have the testosterone to make their muscles grow drastically. You may see slight muscle growth, but lifting this way will only tone you, build muscle strength and increase your metabolism.

During the season, your main goal in the weight room should be to maintain what you have and to condition your muscles. Therefore, you may do lighter weights with higher repetitions. You also will not be working toward exhaustion. During the playing season, with only five days between competitions, you do not always have time to recover and let your muscles rebuild. Therefore, you need to lower the intensity of your workouts and, at some point in your season, you should also reduce the amount of time you spend in the gym. Your goal should be to lift each muscle group once a week. So, lifting two-to-three times per week should be the norm. By that time, you should be changing your emphasis to working on court skills.

As for exercises, here are some for each muscle group. These are just a few examples of sets:

Chest	Triceps	Back	Biceps	Shoulders	Forearms
1. Cable Flies	1. Tricep Pull Down	1. Lat Pull Down	1. Alternate Bicep Curls	1. Military Press	1. Forearm Curls (vary directions)
2. Incline Press	2. French Curl	* vary grips	2. Reverse Bicep Curls	2. Shrugs	2. Grip Machine
3. Dumbbell Pull Over	3. Rope Pull Down	2. Seated Row	3. Hammer Curls	3. Front Raise	3. Forearm Twists
4. Push-ups	4. Reverse Pull Down	3. Rear Deltoid Flies	4. Concentration Curls	4. Lateral Raise	
	5. Kickbacks	4. Hyper—Extensions		5. Upright Row	
	6. Dips			6. Rotator Cuff exercises	

Quads	Hamstrings	Calves	Gluteus	Abductors	Abdominal
1. Leg Extensions	1. Leg Curls	1. Standing Calf Raise	1. Leg Kick Backs	1. Hip Abduction	1. Crunches
2. Squats	2. Reverse Leg Curls	2. Seated Calf Raise		2. Thigh Abduction	2. Side bends
3. Lunges	3. Straight Leg Dead Lift				3. Leg Lifts
4. Leg Press					4. Incline Sit-ups
5. Dead lift					* various exercises

Of course, when you do these exercises you may not do them all. You may find new exercises that you feel work better for you and that are more challenging, or fun. The key is to mix it up. Your muscles will stop responding if you do not change things and you will get bored. If you use new routines, you will stay motivated, which will increase your likelihood of getting to the gym.

For example, a lot of new weight training programs call for the use of a Swiss Ball, so that you are working on your core as you are performing other exercises. Customize your own workout. Take a little time to research these exercises on your own, or hire a trainer at your gym to show you how to perform them correctly. Try new exercises and see how your body responds. Also, keep in mind the notion of "quality over quantity" as you approach your physical training.

As for what to lift when, try to do your lower body workout two times a week. For upper body workouts, lift back, triceps, and shoulders on the same day, and chest, biceps and forearms together.

You should try to mix push exercises with pull exercises. Since you use your shoulders, triceps and back the most of your upper body muscles in volleyball, you should spend two days in the gym for those types of sets, and one day for chest and arms.

You may also want to mix up what you lift on a given day. Some people do not like to lift chest and triceps on the same day because they feel that their chest exercises tire out the triceps, causing them to get little out of their triceps sets, due to the already fatigued muscle. You may opt to lift chest and triceps together, and back and biceps together, to really fire up and fatigue those muscle groups, so that those muscles become stronger when you recover. Authorities on this topic will tell you different things. So, try both routines out and see what you like the best. You can also alternate your muscle group pairings every week or month to prevent muscle boredom.

Conditioning and Quickness

It doesn't matter how strong you are, or how hard you can hit if you can't keep up your effort the whole day. Doubles is a physically trying game. You have to be in shape if you expect to make it through a tournament and some of the conditions that go along with it, such as extreme heat.

As a part of your weight training, you should be doing cardiovascular exercise. Experts say that you do not reap cardiovascular benefits until you have done at least 20 minutes of exercise. Therefore, you should aim to do 30 minutes on the bike, stepper, or elliptical four-five times per week. Coincidentally, 30 minutes matches the length of most games that you will play. You may want to avoid running on the treadmill, because the impact can gradually do damage to your knees.

When you do a cardio session you should incorporate interval training at least half of the time that you perform a cardio session. Interval training means that you will vary your intensity throughout the exercise. Volleyball is a game of short bursts. You may play for ten seconds, then there is some dead time between when the play ends and when the next serve is put into play. So, at the beginning of each minute of exercise, you should sprint the first 10-15 seconds to mimic the bursts of energy you will need in a game. This also keeps your muscles firing by working on fast twitch muscle fibers.

Many experts in the field believe that simply exercising for long distances at the same pace can actually reduce your vertical jump. To avoid this, and to get the most out of your workouts, make your training as much like game conditions as possible. To accomplish that, be sure to incorporate interval training into your workout schedule.

Footwork

It is also important to be quick and agile in your various movements around the court, as well as being conditioned to play. Having good and fast footwork pays off in chasing down a ball, or getting into the proper position to make a dig. It is important to practice movements you may actually use in the game. Here are some exercises you can try:

Footwork Drills

Exercise	Sets/Reps
Sprints	3 sets of 25 yards
Butt Kicks	3 sets of 25 yards
High Step	3 sets of 25 yards
High Knees	3 sets of 25 yards
Carioca	3 sets of 25 yards
Slide	3 sets of 25 yards

Footwork Drills (Continued)

Exercise	Sets/Reps
Power Skip	3 sets of 25 yards
Back Pedal	3 sets of 25 yards
Machine Guns/Fire Feet	3 sets of :30
Ice Skater	3 sets of :30
Dot Drill	3 sets
Left-Right Line Hop	3 sets of :30
Front-Back Line Hop	3 sets of :30
Stutter Step	3 sets of :30
Walking Lunges	3 sets of 20

Once you get accustomed to these basic exercises, challenge yourself by doing ladder exercises. Power Systems sells a ladder for about $65. They also sell a lot of other tools that aid conditioning, such as dot drills and weight vests. You can also obtain more drills online by searching related sites.

You may also find it very helpful to look through online forums and discussion groups. People share their ideas about what works and what does not. You can save yourself a lot of time by reading through other people's experiences. You can get a lot of fresh new ideas for various parts of your workout regimen in this way.

Still another type of footwork you should do reflects game scenarios. Take some time and craft your own drills, based on movements you know that you will be doing a lot in a game. Sometimes, instead of doing the above workout or the ladder workout, be creative and arrange an entire routine based on your court movements.

For example, I know that one major movement I will do is jump serve, then sprint to my defensive position to dig and then transition so I can approach and hit. Therefore, I devise a set where I replicate those exact movements, then do a certain amount of repetitions. Karch Kiraly, an AVP Tour pro, markets a book where he describes his court-conditioning program in full and I highly recommend the book. Not only is he the top winner on the AVP Tour, but also he is also over 40-years-old and still able to compete on the tour because of his superior conditioning. He knows what it takes to train and prepare his body for competition.

Jumping

I knew when I started playing volleyball that I would have to devote a lot of time and energy to improving my vertical jump to be competitive because my height. So I worked hard and improved. In fact, my vertical was a sad 12 inches when I was a junior in high school, but doubled by the time I finished college!

I have tried pretty much everything on the market in order to add inches to my jump. Some things have worked, and some have been scams. It is important for you to realize that increasing your vertical is not an overnight process, as some fad products lead you to believe, nor is it as easy as some of the advertisements claim. When you see ads that say their product will increase your vertical six to ten inches in three months, or that if you wear a special sole in your shoe you will gain some extra inches, do not believe the hype. If it seems too good to be true, it probably is rubbish. All great plyometric programs require a rigid schedule, basic strength requirements and a serious long-term commitment in order to work effectively. So do not buy a product unless it comes with an exercise program.

Before you start a jump training or plyometric program, you should also know that it is not for everyone and not everyone will have the same results. A person can only benefit from certain types of jump training if he or she has adequate leg strength. Otherwise, he or she can risk damage.

A good rule of thumb for high-intensity jump training is that you should be able to squat your own weight. Before you start, make sure you have done some sort of light plyometric exercises. Also, everyone's body responds differently. Some people can build fast twitch muscle fibers and explosiveness more easily than others. Some athletes are more naturally gifted. I am sure you have seen many athletes who seem to be able to jump out of the gym, only to find out later that that athlete does not work on jumping ability at all.

Each athlete is unique, so don't compare yourself to others. Be patient as you train and make sure you can commit to a program. If you do this, you will see results at your own pace. It will usually take three months before you see a noticeable gain and six months before you see big progress.

You can do two different types of training. The first is low impact plyometrics. These exercises mimic jumps you do in a game, such as block jumps and approach jumps. They do not put a huge strain on your muscles. The best way to increase your jump is by jumping. So, low impact jumps might be a good place to start.

The second type of training, which is more advanced, includes higher intensity and impact exercises. A common example of this type of exercise is a "depth jump." In this exercise, you jump off an elevated platform of at least 18 inches and then immediately explode back up when you contact the ground. Other programs are the "Strength Shoes" or the "Jump Soles" programs, which both require the use of a special shoe. In these programs, half of your foot is on a platform and the heel of your foot is unsupported. This places a special emphasis on your calves, making them work harder.

Some critics say that you do not need to have this type of shoe to train effectively. There have been studies that have compared users of "jump shoes" with people who did plyometric exercises without the shoes. Both groups made gains and there was no significant difference, although the group that wore the specialized shoes did have a slight edge.

Ultimately, your quads are the area you want to make explosive, as they are most involved in creating an explosive jump. Therefore, it cannot hurt if you use the shoes while performing certain exercises, as long as you follow the product guidelines. In reading online forums, there are a lot of people that have claimed that these elevated soles have caused them ankle and Achilles heel problems. I have not experienced this using the product, as prescribed. Again, this comes with making sure that your body is fully prepared to start a high impact regimen.

In fact, I have tried depth jump training, "strength shoes" and low impact programs. All have worked for me, and all have drawbacks. I suggest starting out with low impact jump training to pave the way for harder exercises. While doing these type exercise you will notice some gains in your vertical for the first couple of months, but those gains will gradually level. At that point, you will experience increased tone and conditioning. This means you will be able to jump the same throughout the whole day at tournaments without a lot of recovery time.

If you elect to do depth jump training, you will need a lot of rest in between workouts and will need to figure out how to fit this time into your playing schedule. However, it will add power and explosiveness to your jump. Like with any program, you need to mix things up. It is easy to hit a plateau.

If you decide to mix it up by training with special shoes, I would highly recommend "Strength Shoes" over "Jump Soles." Although they are a little more expensive, you do not need to worry about adjusting them continually throughout your workout. One great thing about the program is there are three levels, depending on where you are in your training. It also comes with a video that details each exercise.

There is a long recovery time with this workout as well. Even if you have been doing plyometric training for several years prior to getting the shoes, you should put yourself on the beginner program because it will challenge you. After you do a workout with the "strength shoes," you will feel the fatigue in your legs. Usually it takes two full days in between each workout to fully recover. If you find this happening to you, make sure to include lots of protein in your diet. This will help your muscles recover faster so that you can train more.

One great thing about "Strength Shoes" is the program's versatility. All sorts of exercises can be done while wearing the shoes. Even though Strength Shoes has its own program, you can use the shoes in conjunction with any program. You can go through your usual routine, but wearing the shoes, which makes your low impact jump training more challenging. You can also do depth jump exercises with the shoes on, so you are working your quads and your calves. Likewise, you can wear them during footwork and agility exercises to mix things up and challenge your muscles. Just be careful not to overdo it. It is very easy to injure yourself, as the combination of high intensity exercises and added stress on your calves can create instability.

The intent in going over these products is not to endorse or authorize any certain jump training program or product, but rather to raise awareness about the pros and cons of plyometric aids that are currently on the market. What I will advise you is you can get started with low impact jumps. You can do all of these jumps with or without special shoes, but I strongly recommend if you are serious about increasing your vertical that you do invest in that type of product. You should also prepare your body physically to do some of the higher intensity exercises.

Here are some examples:

Low Impact Jump Training Exercises (3 sets of 10)
Always start with a five-minute run and stretch

- Standing Vertical Jump

- Block Jump

- Tuck Jump

- Squat Jump (one of the best exercises for increasing your vertical)

- Pogo Jumps (just using your ankles)

- Split Squat Jump

- Approach Jump

- Long Jump

- Jump ups (onto an 18" platform or chair)

- Power Step ups (onto an 18" platform or chair, alternating legs to explode upward off the platform)

Cool down with a five-minute run and stretch

Make sure that if you have a competition that you are not doing plyometrics the day before, as your muscle fibers will be broken down. You also should work on strengthening your abdominal muscles and stretching your hip flexors, as those are often overlooked elements in increasing you jump. In general, it is good to have a stretching routine and incorporate it every day you train to maximize your gains and minimize the chance of injury. If you go to my reference and resource page, you can find a list of recommended literature to read on these subjects, as well as where to buy some of these products.

Pre-Game Diet

I am not one to tell someone else how, or what, to eat. There are obvious things that every serious athlete should avoid—such as soda, sugars, junk food and alcohol. There are also obvious things each athlete needs in their diet—such as protein.

Many athletes treat food as fuel. They do not go for taste, but rather aim to give their body all the nutrients it needs. In my playing experience, I am not sure how much impact a person's diet makes. But, eating correctly certainly does not hurt. However, I have seen many volleyball players primarily eat pizza, or other fast food and do quite well. I have also seen athletes with low body fat and who really watch what they eat not do very well.

My philosophy is that a person, athlete or not, needs to find a healthy balance. It is mainly important that a person does not take in more calories than they can burn off in a day. You also want to be careful about ruining the progress you made in the gym with bad eating habits.

While I will not preach about what to eat on a daily basis, largely because I am not a dietician and because I, too, am guilty of splurging on junk food, I will say that what you eat the day before and the day of a tournament is important. This is because it does have an effect on how you feel which directly affects your performance.

I never eat a lot on tournament days. I tend to be very anxious and prefer not to have a lot of food in my stomach. This gives more room in there to the butterflies! What I have found over the years is that by not eating, especially on hot days, it was harder to keep my focus and energy. I may not eat a lot on tournament days, but I have found a way to get the important nutrients in without weighing myself down.

The night before a tournament, eat a meal packed with carbohydrates—such as whole-wheat pasta. Your body stores the carbohydrates and they are ready to be burned off the next day to help you sustain your energy. Also, the day of the tournament make sure to eat or bring some of the following items:

Food	Purpose
Oatmeal	Fills you up
Vitamin Water	Hydrates and provides needed vitamins you may not be getting from food
Dill Pickles	The vinegar helps stave off dehydration and cramps
Nuts	Protein, energy, and salt to help retain water
Banana and Peanut Butter	Potassium helps fight off cramps and peanut butter has protein. The simple sugars can provide a quick energy burst.

The ideal snack during the day is a carbohydrate with a fat. Half of a bagel with peanut butter or cream cheese would be an ideal snack. Adding a piece of fruit is also a good idea. After a tournament, continue to drink water to prevent any cramps that may occur at night, as well as to have some source of protein to aid muscle rebuilding.

It should be common sense, but alcohol is not a part of a successful athlete's diet. Neither is caffeine or other chemicals that will only dehydrate you. Foods that have a high amount of sugars should also be avoided.

Practice Makes Perfect

It is important to have some base strength, a decent vertical jump and good cardiovascular stamina. Athletes train themselves year-round to develop these things. You do need to tone down the heavy lifting and high impact plyometrics once you get into your playing season. Nothing trains you better to be a good player than to play often. As you near the start of your season, make it a point to replace some lifting and plyometric sessions with court drills, like serving, hitting and serve receive.

Try to play as many pickup games as you can and focus on certain elements of your game that you want to keep sharp. So, for example, if you want to work on your shots, play a whole game without hitting and work on your placement and court vision to see where your opponents are playing defense.

You should also try to get court time for drills. As I said earlier, make a commitment to buy your own net and balls. Take the time to practice your serves and work on placing your hits and passing the ball. Getting a feel for the ball and the basic movements you will have to make can have a big payoff in a tournament.

Final Thoughts

As you begin to plan your workouts, remember that more is not always better. Bodies need time to recover and you do not want to burn yourself out. Make a schedule that will develop core strength, conditioning, and your vertical jump. The schedule should be something you can commit to and something that is challenging, yet fun. You can always do more if you feel your body can take it. Also, feel free to change your workouts. Muscles get used to routine and the mind gets bored! Your priorities also will change as you improve, so you may also want to change the emphasis of your workouts.

9

It's All In Your Head—Preparing Mentally

Have you ever wondered why the most athletic people do not always win? Have you ever seen a good player lose to a lesser opponent? Ever heard the expression that the game is 10 percent physical, 90 percent mental?

If you have been around sports, there is a good chance you have heard all of the above. The reason why is that most athletes prepare themselves physically, but overlook the importance of preparing for the competition mentally. That's because fundamentals are your foundation, strength and conditioning are what brings you the victories, but a strong mental game is needed in order for a player to reach the apex and stay there. In this chapter, I will discuss the things that every doubles player should think about before a competition, as well as some things that I have found particularly effective.

Setting Goals

The first thing that any player should do before entering a competition is to set goals. You should focus on what you want to achieve.

Then, you can focus on how you are going to reach those aspirations.

You may have a simple goal of having a winning record, or beating a certain team that you usually can't beat. It may be to reach the finals, and maybe then to win. It may not even be result-oriented. For example, your goal may be to work on playing defense better behind a block. No matter how good you may be, it is vital to set goals for yourself. Even though Misty May is considered the best defensive player on the beach, she got a new coach this season to target areas of her defensive game she thought needed improvement. Having a measurable goal will keep you focused on your own success and give you something for which to strive.

Another reason to set goals is that it allows you to be successful, even if your team loses that day. For instance, even if you are a player who normally reaches finals, you might want to put a limit on how many points your opponents will score. The emphasis of your goal should always be to reach beyond prior accomplishment and focus on showing progress.

Whatever goals you set, however, should be realistic. If you have never won a game in Open before, your goal should not be to win the tournament. Set goals that are challenging and only slightly out of reach. That way you need to work to meet your goals. There is something very powerful about exceeding expectations and growing as a player. Each time you play, you should reevaluate your goals and tweak them as you experience success. You also need to be analytical and identify your limitations so that you can eliminate them. Even the best players have weaknesses. If you can be truthful with yourself and identify your own, this will go a long way to help you become a better player. Some athletes naturally continue to practice what they are already good at because it is safe, and shy away from what they are weak at out of frustration and because it may not be "fun." Although there is much to be said for fine-tuning, you cannot ignore glaring weak spots.

Setting goals should not only be limited to competitions. When doubles season ends, you should reflect on the year and set goals for what you want to work on during the off-season. As an example, you may decide that you want to work on your vertical jump. Finally, before the doubles season starts again, you should list three things you hope to accomplish before the season ends. These goals are two fold and include focusing on what you want to achieve as well as improving identified weaknesses of your game. In fact, goal setting and monitoring should be an ongoing process throughout your playing career.

Once you set your goals, you need to plan a course of action. If your goal is to increase your vertical jump, simply having it as a goal is not going to make it happen. You need to think about how you will reach that goal. That will involve reading some literature on plyometrics and developing a routine. Finally, it will take a long-term commitment to training with a plyometric program. Take some time now to set some goals for yourself and think about how you will make them happen. Be specific and feel free to continue your thoughts on additional paper if necessary.

Season Goals	How you will accomplish the goal
1.	1.
2.	2.
3.	3.

Off-Season Goals	How you will accomplish the goal

1.	1.
2.	2.
3.	3.

Game Planning

To accomplish your goals you will have prepare for competition, not just physically, but strategically. For a game or tournament, a team should always have some sort of plan of attack that takes into account their strengths and their opponents' weaknesses. You need to figure out how you will defend your court and attack your opponents' court—how you will avoid your opponents' strengths and expose their weaknesses.

Volleyball groups in most areas tend to be a pretty tight-knit community. Usually you know 90 percent of the competition. The main changes in strategy occur when someone switches partners and you need to adjust for the new partnership. For example, you might have always served a player because they pass poorly. Then, that player changes partners and is now playing with someone who can run down those balls and put up good sets. The new partner was someone that, in the past, you preferred not to serve. The new partnership poses a dilemma for you. Therefore, you need to come up with a new game plan.

Developing a "Plan B" is also important. A couple of years ago, I was playing in the Pottstown Rumble. It is one of the largest grass doubles tournaments in the nation. The pool I was placed in was very competitive and, with only two teams breaking, a team could not afford to lose many games. In our second-to-last match of pool, we faced a team that was a pretty solid beach team. The original plan was to serve the shorter player. She was an excellent passer, but very predictable on offense.

We started out the game with this in mind, but then the other team seemingly adjusted. They started to use the "on two" offense. The taller player began taking every ball over on two, instead of setting. She got some awesome swings because her partner had such great ball control. They wound up chipping away the lead and, at one point, going ahead.

Once that occurred, we called a time out. We decided that we could not let the better offensive player continue to hit without having to work for the set. So, we drew up "Plan B." It turns out that all the teams served the shorter player, while her partner hit on two. So our game plan played right into our opponents' comfort area.

When we started to serve the taller player, who rarely passed, the team was not ready. It completely threw them off their game. We went on to win the first game, and easily won the next game, 15-3, which propelled us into the playoffs.

The moral here is, eventually, teams will get used to what you throw at them. A good team will adjust. Therefore, you have to have some alternatives and be able to adjust your original mindset, in case your original game plan does not work.

If you travel to play and are not familiar with the competition, planning for the other team will be difficult in advance. Then, you will have to shift your focus to your team and how you will play. Then you must learn as much about your opponent as you can the day of the tournament by watching.

When you think about your game plan, there is a thought process you should follow. First, always think about you and your partner. Based on your strengths, which of you will be the aggressive server, who will block, and who should take more court, etc.? Obviously, if you play with the same partner all the time, this shouldn't be a concern. Whatever the case, you should aim to maximize the individual skills on your team so that the team can perform at its best.

Next, you want to think about your opponent, considering their strengths and weaknesses. Some questions you may want to consider:

- Where do they like to serve?
- Who is the better passer?
- Who is the better hitter?
- Do they have shots and if so, which ones?
- Who is the better setter?
- Is there an area they leave open or poses them problems on defense?
- What types of serves give them the most problems?
- Should we block?

Based on these answers, you then can come up with a plan. For example, if one player is a weak passer, you, obviously, plan to serve that person more, or all, of the balls. However, if both players are strong passers, you have to decide who is the weaker hitter. Or, you may need to figure out where to serve them that would make their transition to offense the hardest. Depending on the strength of your opponent, a simple adjustment may give you the edge.

You also need to plan your defense. The main thing you need to think about is whether your team will block and, if so, who will carry the blocking duties and what area will the block try to take. There may be times when you decide not to block against a team, since you may have more success digging. Even so, you will have to put a block up against some teams you face if their offense is so strong they sideout every time on an empty net.

As you get to know a team, you might start to see tendencies develop. It is valuable to key in on the trends of your opponent. Some players do a certain shot the first time they see a block. It may be just a knee-jerk reaction, but knowing they tend to do that shot may earn you an extra point.

Other players have a tendency to swing around the block, rather than hit over the block, to an empty spot. Pay attention to this when you observe teams because this information can create more opportunities for you when you play against these teams. You can use this information to help you make decisions about where to play on defense and to help you get a jump on the ball.

Another reason why you should think about how you want to play in advance is because, as you plan, you are actually playing out the game in your head. Visualization is a powerful tool used by many world-class athletes to enhance their performance.

Visualization and Cues

I am not an expert on visualization, or things of the sort. However, I have read a few books and have used some strategies successfully. I will give you a few tips and drills here. I'd suggest you try them out and, if they work for you, I strongly suggest you buy a book on this topic. I think you will find the few exercises I give you valuable enough that you will want to try more for yourself.

I never used visualization in my training until I was in the sport for five or six years. One day I picked up a book called The Mental Edge, by Kenneth Baum, which I highly recommend. Baum brought up many sports-related anecdotes.

One anecdote, in particular, really caught my attention. It was a story about a skier who had a major injury that forced him to miss almost a year of competition. He couldn't even train. What this skier could do, however, was visualize himself skiing and going through the motions. His first time back on the mountains was at a competition. He did not have time to prepare or practice the course. However, he had spent so much time visualizing himself making all the turns on that course that his mind made a connection with his body. In that way, he had familiarized himself with the slope and turns of the mountain. That day, he set a personal course record (Baum & Trubo, 1999).

It turns out there has been numerous studies done on the impact of visualization on athletic performance. In one study, it was found that there was actually chemical activity going on in the nerves while this visualization was done and that a body would respond as if it was actually doing whatever the person was visualizing! So, heart rates rose, or subjects of the study perspired, just as they would in a real competition (Baum & Trubo, 1999).

At first I did not believe these findings. But, as I thought back, I remembered that there were times in my life that I had visualized myself making a play. Then, surprisingly, things seemed to work out in real life, just as I had seen them play out in my head. This happened for both good and bad outcomes.

When I became interested in learning more about doubles, I did not even think about the importance of mental strength. I read virtually every topic on conditioning, plyometrics, strength training and basic skills. Then one day, I came across a book that promised to enhance physical skills by using the power of imagination, created by visualization. I figured, the book only cost eight bucks, what could it hurt?

As I read, it became clear to me that my mental game was truly having an adverse effect on my actual game. There were so many times I recalled that I unnecessarily made myself nervous about passing a hard jump serve. Right before the serve, I was filled with negative thoughts about getting aced. I actually paralyzed myself with nervousness. As I continued to read, I realized the importance of disregarding negative thoughts and replacing them with positive ones.

By thinking negatively, you set yourself up for failure. An athlete needs to attack the game by changing their thinking, and then there will be a noticeable difference is skill execution, comfort level and confidence. I began to work on my visualization skills and, after I tried an exercise, I saw immediate results. The power of the mind is incredible. The best thing is that most exercises can be used on the court, in the heat of the moment, or off the court.

Eventually, I started "daydreaming" about playing the next day. I could feel myself getting nervous like I usually do the day of the competition. I would also picture myself playing against a certain team, or having a really nice hit. Sometimes, I even envisioned being down 10 points and then played out a personal highlight reel of how I would come back to win.

At some point, I am sure you have all done this. Somehow, when I got into the situation the next day, I already had a script for how I would react. I found I was calmer and had more confidence. Although, in reality, I might not have executed a certain play before or beaten a particular team, I had done it in my head. This was enough to make me interested in learning more. I immediately saw the value of this and made it a goal to incorporate specific visualization exercises into my weekly regimen.

Here are some techniques I have found to be pretty effective:

Scripting. Think of a situation you could be in during a tournament. See yourself overcoming adversity and having success. It is important in a visualization to focus on images and sensations beyond yourself. Think about the sounds you would be hearing, how your partner would respond, how the other team would be reacting, and etcetera. Focus on how you are feeling and what you are doing (Baum & Trubo, 1999).

For example, let's say you've had trouble passing a certain player's serve. Envision that player serving their toughest serves, you knowing where they are all going to go and, then, passing each of them up perfectly. Imagine how the ball feels coming off your arms. Notice the look on the server's face after you pass what should have been an ace.

The best part about this technique is that it can be used before and during a tournament. There have been many times in a game when I went back to the serving line, pictured where I wanted my serve to land and imagined myself executing the serve. It took less than five seconds to do. Then, when I actually served, it went exactly where I imagined. Try it, then don't be surprised if things on court play out just like you planned them.

Highlight Montage. This is a confidence-building visualization. Every athlete goes though periods of self-doubt. A player might be convinced that they are bad at defense. Because of that belief, they might actually start playing poor defense.

In reality, that player may have the ability to play well, but may be in a rut. That player should create a personal mental montage of their greatest defensive moments. In this visualization, the player should replay in their head the hard hits they have gotten up, the diving digs, and awesome reads they have made in the past. What this does is build the athlete's self-image and shows that the athlete has done it and can do it (Baum & Trubo, 1999).

Drawing from personal success can help you overcome slumps you may experience. You can run these highlight reels in your head during a game to spark some confidence when you need it.

Make-Believe. One way to play better is to constantly try to act like players you admire. Remember the ad campaign, "Like Mike" and all the little kids on the basketball courts sticking out their tongues as they did a lay-up? Your goal, when you visualize, is to duplicate the posture, mannerisms, qualities and thoughts of the athlete you most admire. We have all done this as kids, so why stop pretending now?

It is one of the easier mental exercises to do because it just involves watching others and then patterning yourself after them and their actions and behaviors. When you do this, concentrate on how your role model performs. Notice his/her expressions, body posture, the attitude and aura he/she brings to the playing field.

If your role model is a person you know or see on television, study this person carefully. How do they walk onto the court? What do they do while waiting to receive the serve? How do they carry themselves? How do they react to a good play or a bad play? Then, imagine yourself taking on those characteristics. Close your eyes and picture yourself assuming that athlete's posture, facial expression, etc. Try to model yourself after this person (Baum & Trubo, 1999).

Fast Forward/Time Machine. During a lull in the game, imagine how the next play will go. For instance, if you find yourself getting tight about passing, run the next point in your head. As the other team is getting ready to serve, actually envision the serve coming to you and then picture positioning yourself in front of the ball and making a clean, crisp pass. Usually, how you play it out seconds before the serve is exactly how it happens in real time. It seems simple, but give it a try. I am sure you will be amazed at the results.

These are just a couple examples to try. See if they work for you and, if so, tweak them to meet your needs. If, at first you are having some difficulty keeping your focus, do not worry. Like any other skill, it takes practice to use it effectively.

Another thing to remember is to keep your visualizations positive in nature. Make time for this in your training and treat it as a priority. It is something simple that you can do while you are exercising, or as you are getting ready for bed and it has the potential to make a huge difference in your game—as hopefully you will see.

The Right Attitude

Attitude is everything, as they say in sports. I truly believe that. Your approach to any situation—on or off the court—has a huge impact to how that situation turns out. Your outlook will determine your success in future similar situations. Ken Baum, the author of <u>The Mental Edge</u>, starts his book by listing 10 perception stretchers. Read these over and reflect on them. Post the list some place where you can see it everyday.

1. *A loss becomes a gain.* If you do lose, as athletes will at some point in their career, take something positive out of it. Figure out what it is that made you come up short and then work on it. Life is too short to make the same mistakes twice. Examine your approach and make changes (Baum & Trubo, 1999).

2. *If you do what you've always done, you'll get what you have always gotten.* Every player goes through a rut and hits plateaus. When that happens, you need to change what you are doing. If you do not do anything differently, then you should not expect to get different results. Being able to change is the key to increasing performance (Baum & Trubo, 1999).

3. *The imagination is more powerful than the will.* Using visualization and letting your imagination run wild opens up a world of possibilities. Decades ago, a collegiate coach dreamt of his

team's hitters already being in the air before the setter had the ball and being able to surprise the defense with a quick set. That is where the middle quick offense came from and it rapidly changed the game of volleyball. There are many ways to win a game. The right way is the way that works, and for each team that is different. So, use your imagination and be creative (Baum & Trubo, 1999).

4. *Bodies work perfectly; the mind gets in the way.* Baum mentioned a phrase, "Paralysis by Analysis." This is when athletes psych themselves out to such an extent that they cannot physically perform a skill. If you think you are going to shank a pass, most likely you will. If you think you are a bad player, you probably will play poorly. So, think positively. If you make this shift, you will see an immediate difference (Baum & Trubo, 1999).

5. *Limitations are temporary.* Every player has weaknesses. The best ones work hard to overcome them. California Angels' pitcher Jim Abbott only had one hand, but that did not stop him from throwing a no-hitter in the major leagues. He found a way to maneuver his glove during play so that he could throw and catch using the same arm. If you keep working, you will improve (Baum & Trubo, 1999).

6. *Anyone can play any sport better.* Through weight training, jump training and conditioning you can improve your game. Even the best players can improve. That is why Misty May and Kerri Walsh keep practicing and working on their game to keep it sharp, even though they have been the number one-ranked team in the world for the last few years. They still want to be more dominant and they know that the tier of players just below them are working extra hard to knock off the champs (Baum & Trubo, 1999).

7. *Events have no meaning besides what you give them.* Why is it that a player gets more nervous on game point? The pressure is higher. The problem is this pressure is created by the player. The best players are the ones that are "clutch" at the key moments. That is because they do not create this pressure in their heads. They do not perceive a difference between passing the first serve of the game, or the last. They realize that if they killed their first set, then they can make the same play on game point. Each point should be treated equally and played the same way. This is how the best players approach the game. When a player starts to put more meaning on one part of the game, they are adding unneeded pressure (Baum & Trubo, 1999).

8. *Getting better is more important than winning.* The goal is to win, but the most important thing is improving. Making personal progress is really the only thing that is a true measure of your accomplishments. You might have won the last three tournaments you have played in, but in the next tournament, there could be two teams from out of state that are solid teams. Losing to them does not mean you are a bad player (Baum & Trubo, 1999).

9. *Practice like you play.* If you are lazy and not intense in practice it will carry over to the game. When you practice, your mind and body makes connections. If you do not make solid connections, they will not be there when you need them. How can you expect to focus and get pumped up in a match if you have not played like that in preparation (Baum & Trubo, 1999)?

10. *The more you expect from a situation, the more you will achieve.* Why is it that the cockiest players tend to always finish first? It is because they expect to win. Players who have low expecta-

tions do not strive to succeed and that is why they often do not (Baum & Trubo, 1999). Most people reach the expectations they set for themselves and become their own self-fulfilling prophecy. So why not set the bar higher?

* Perception Stretchers from: Baum, Ken. <u>The Mental Edge.</u>

Think about these 10 ideas often. Remember to stay positive and keep your expectations high. Realize that preparing mentally is just as important as preparing physically—so, make time for it. I hope that you find some of these ideas helpful and that you come to learn the value of some of these techniques and incorporate them into your training.

10

Epilogue

Hopefully, as you make these philosophies, strategies and techniques part of your game, you will start to experience success. Your goal should always be to get better and reach new heights. If you are playing A, your goal should be getting up to AA, and so on and so forth. There will be setbacks, but do not forget to see the lesson in every loss. Be patient as you grow as a player, and recognize things you are doing right and take pride in those things. Identify what weaknesses are holding you back and work at making those your strengths.

In time you should be able to move up to the next level, or start winning at the level you are currently at now. Realize that as you grow as a player, you may outgrow your partner. You and your partner might be a great team and hide weaknesses at one level, but not at a higher level. If this winds up being the case, you will have to either commit to improving as a team or make the choice to find a partner who you may have more success with.

Many players have a difficult time coming to this decision. First, it is hard to end a partnership. But, even professionals end partnerships when they hit plateaus. Karch Kiraly, the most winning player in the history of the AVP Tour, has made several partner changes in his career. He even split with partner Kent Steffes, despite long tournament winning streaks. Remember, it is just a part of the game and is in no way personal.

Second, finding a partner in a higher level to take a chance on you is hard to do. People who are already successful grow accustomed to it. They do not want to risk a lesser finish or take the time to learn how to play with someone new. So, for a player trying to move up the ranks, it can be hard to improve without the right partner.

Ideally, you should be able to play with the same partner throughout a season. But, teams hit plateaus, just like players. So, how do you get a higher-skilled player to take a chance on you?

Sometimes, it is a case of being in the right place at the right time. Rachel Wacholder got her big break when Misty May decided at the last minute that she could not play, due to injury. This left Kerri Walsh, arguably the best player in the world at the time, without a partner. Walsh and Wacholder teamed up and won the tournament. They went on to win a couple more tournaments that same summer as May was recovering. Shortly after that, Wacholder was fielding calls from other players on the tour. Eventually, she wound up partnering with the #3 ranked player, Elaine Youngs.

This probably does not happen often, so you need to create your own opportunities by increasing your exposure. Become part of the circle. Start playing at the level you want to do well in, even if, initially, you may not be able to win it or break pool. Let people start to see what you can do. Showcase your skills and play hard. It will attract some attention.

Ask a veteran who plays that level to play with you. Physically, they may be past their prime, but, mentally, they can still outsmart opponents and they will bring confidence and composure to the team.

They will also teach you a lot about the other players at that level. While teams may pick on you during the game, your partner, because of the experience factor, will be a rock and able to provide consistency. This will enable you to play your game without worrying about them playing their game. You will eventually start to place better. As you do, you will have more and more people respecting your game and wanting to play with you.

Before I leave you with what is, hopefully, many new ideas, I want to urge you to make a commitment to improving your game. Although it will help drive you, all the wanting and knowledge in the world will not by itself make you successful. You have to work!

Make the time commitment to conditioning your body and mind. Spend the money to make yourself better. Spend the $1,000 necessary on the equipment you need to give yourself an extra boost. It'll be an investment you can reuse year after year. Most people will spend that much money a year on fast food, gambling, clothing, movies or video games, so, why not make a one time investment in what you love the most and yourself as a player? If you do not do it, no one else will!

Spend the money once and you can work on improving your game for years. Buy a net, five or six balls, a nice pair of sunglasses, a gym membership, and a book or program on plyometrics, conditioning and visualization. You can even split the costs with your partner.

Your preparation is the one aspect of the game you control, so make sure you do not put forth anything less than your best effort. There will always be players that may be better, but NEVER let another player outwork you! And, remember to keep up with the newest literature and research.

Now that you have this wealth of information, start putting it to use. I wish you all the success as you start your quest to becoming a better player. Do not forget to have fun and remember that a little hard work goes a long way. Now that you know what it takes, if you embrace those ideas as keystones as you try to improve, you will guide yourself on a sure path to accomplishment and success.

References and Resources

References

Baum, Kenneth and Trubo, Richard. <u>The Mental Edge: Maximize Your Sports Potential with the Mind-Body Connection</u>. New York: The Berkeley Publishing Group, 1999.

Chu, Donald. <u>Jumping Into Plyometrics</u>. United States: Human Kinetics, 1992.

Johnson, Earvin. <u>My Life</u>. New York: Random House, 1993.

Web Resources

<u>Physical Preparation</u>
Strength Training Exercises and Philosophies
http://www2.gsu.edu/~wwwfit/strength.html

Intro to Plyometric Training
http://www.bodybuilding.com/fun/bbinfo.php?page=Plyometrics

<u>Skills</u>
Tom Wilson's Volleyball Web Site
http://www.volleyballfiles.com

<u>Products</u>
Strength Shoes and other Plyometric Training Aids
http://www.strength-systems.com/

<u>Places to Play</u>
AVP Tour
http://www.avp.com

Capital District Grass Doubles
http://www.cdgd.org

Mike Daly's East Coast Volleyball Page
http://www.geocities.com/colosseum/loge/5057/maininfo.htm

Northwest Volleyball Doubles Tournaments
http://www.volleyballnw.com/SummerOutdoor/default.htm

USA Volleyball
http://www.usavolleyball.org

These websites should get you started, but you can also use www.google.com to find whatever other information you need.

Finally, here's one last bit of advice: NEVER stop learning and you will ALWAYS keep improving your game!

978-0-595-45863-9
0-595-45863-7

Printed in the United States
97420LV00001B/129/A